T0044204

TITANIC

SHIP OF DREAMS

RMS *TITANIC*'S SEA TRIALS, 6 AM ON TUESDAY, APRIL 2, 1912

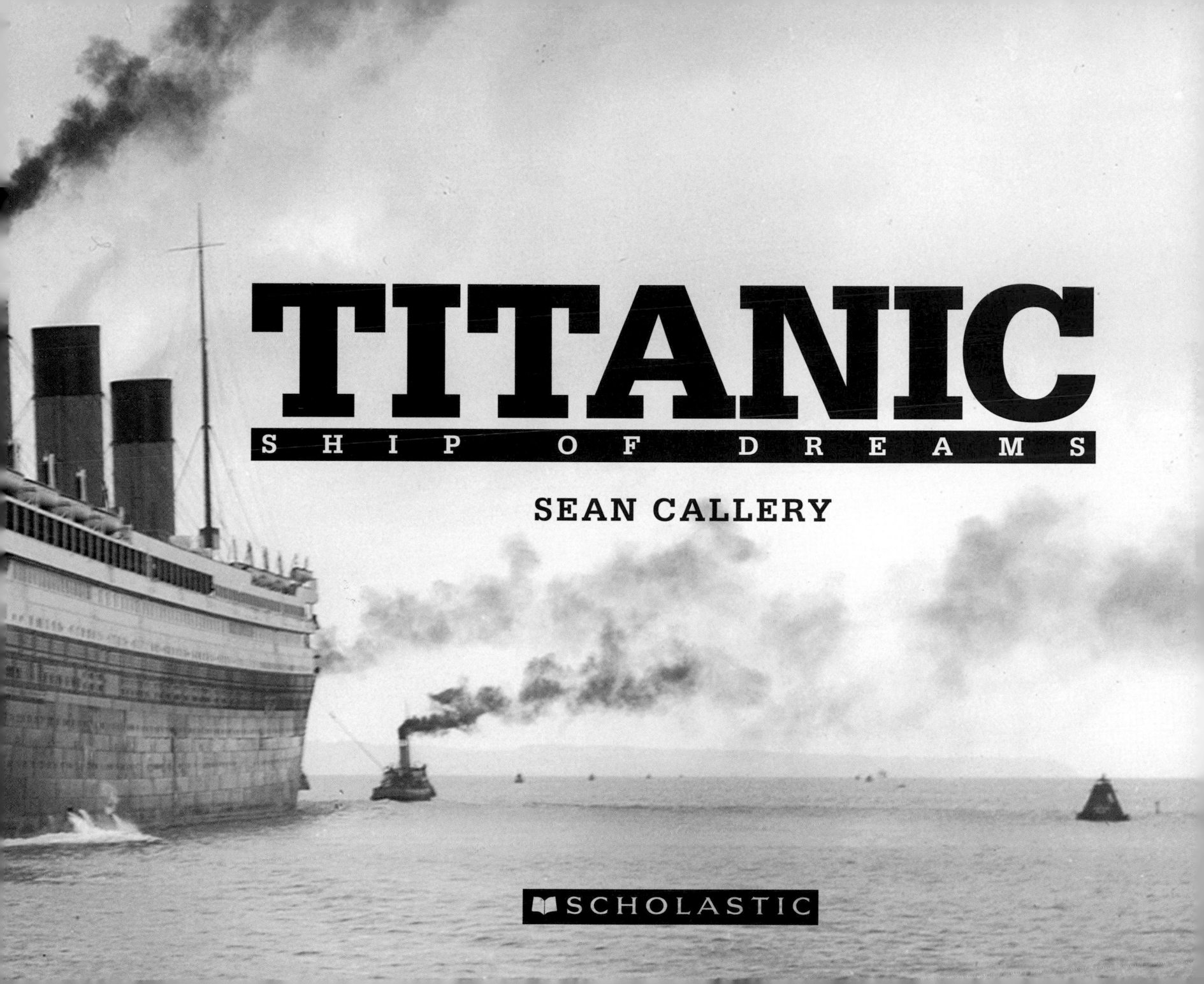

TITANIC

SHIP OF DREAMS

SEAN CALLERY

SCHOLASTIC

Titanic's tragedy

This photograph was taken on the morning of April 15, 1912, from *RMS Carpathia*. Lifeboat 6 is crowded with probably 23 survivors of the *Titanic*'s shipwreck. There was room in the boat for 65 people.

Consultant: Dr. Eric Kentley
Literacy Consultant: Barbara Russ, 21st Century Community Learning Center Director for Winooski (Vermont) School District
UK Editor: Miriam Farbey
US Editor: Ingrid Paredes
Art Director: Bryn Walls
Cover Director: Julia Sabbagh
DTP: John Goldsmid

"I have never seen anything so magnificent, even in a first-class hotel. I might be living in a palace."
—ARTHUR GEE, FIRST-CLASS PASSENGER

Copyright © 2014 by Scholastic Inc.

All rights reserved. Published by Scholastic Inc., *Publishers since 1920*. SCHOLASTIC, and associated logos are trademarks and/or registered trademarks of Scholastic Inc.

No part of this publication may be reproduced, stored in a retrieval system, or transmitted in any form or by any means, electronic, mechanical, photocopying, recording, or otherwise, without the written permission of the publisher. For information regarding permission, write to Scholastic Inc., Attention: Permissions Department, 557 Broadway, New York, NY 10012.

ISBN 978-1-338-79477-9

10 9 8 7 6 5 4 3 24 25 26

China 84
This edition first printing, January 2022.

Scholastic is constantly working to lessen the environmental impact of our manufacturing processes. To view our industry-leading paper procurement policy, visit www.scholastic.com/paperpolicy.

***TITANIC*'S BOILERS, IN THE HARLAND AND WOLFF SHIPYARD**

Contents

Unsinkable giant 8
Sea and be seen 10

Crossing the Atlantic

The ship of dreams 14
Story of a disaster 16
Ship technology 18
Transatlantic rivals 20
Promenaders 22
Immigration 24
Iceberg ahead! 26

Building the ship

Shipbuilding 30
Keel to hull 32
The workforce 34
Powerhouse 36
Preparations 38
Decks 1–5 40
Decks 6–10 42
Safety 44

The voyage

Setting off 48
First class 50
First-class berths 52
Second class 54
Third class 56
Deck to deck 58
Crew 60
Cargo 62
A day on *Titanic* 64
Child's play 66
Navigation 68
Countdown to disaster 70

Sunk

Ice monster 74
Damage 76
In distress 78
The last lifeboat 80
All alone 82
Final moments 84
Last chance 86

Lost and found

Rescued 90
Families fear the worst 92
Saved and lost 94
Heroes and villains 96
Big questions 98
Found 100
At rest 102
Survivors 104
Glossary 106
Index 109
Credits and acknowledgments 112

Unsinkable giant

Titanic became the largest ship in the world when it was completed in 1912. These workers—dwarfed by the giant propellers of *Titanic*'s near-identical sister ship, *Olympic*—thought, as did many people at the time, that the mighty vessels were the safest ever.

Sea and be seen

Titanic had broad decks where passengers—like these second-class guests—could stroll. To avoid spoiling the view, the first-class promenades were kept clear of lifeboats. Although Titanic had more lifeboats than the regulations required, there were not enough to carry all the passengers.

Crossi
Atla

* Which shipping lines competed for passengers?
* Where was *Titanic* carrying passengers to?
* What did promenaders do for exercise?

ng the
ntic

The ship of dreams

Titanic was already a famous ship in 1912. Then, four days into its first voyage, it became the world's most famous shipwreck. The tragedy, with its cast of millionaires and immigrants, and the story of the long search for the wreck captivate us to this day.

The *Titanic* legend

Dramatic accounts of *Titanic*'s last moments, and of its heroes and villains, have been retold many times over the years, in many media.

THE BRITISH FILM *A NIGHT TO REMEMBER* (1958)

JAMES CAMERON'S BLOCKBUSTER (1997)

At the movies

Movie director James Cameron visited *Titanic*'s wreck on the seabed. For his 1997 film, *Titanic*, Cameron used his footage of the wreck and meticulously re-created the ship and its sinking.

Unsinkable

Titanic was the largest and most luxurious ship in the world. This vast iron and steel construction represented a high point in British manufacturing. It carried the most current technology, such as radio and electrical equipment. And, according to the owners, the watertight doors made it unsinkable.

Maiden voyage

Titanic sailed from Southampton at noon on Wednesday, April 10, 1912. As it pulled away from the shore, its enormous propellers sucked another ship out of its berth. The two ships almost collided, to the alarm of *Titanic*'s passengers.

Arguments

People are still debating the disaster and what caused it. Was it human or mechanical error? Why did *Titanic* sail into an ice field at high speed? Why weren't there enough lifeboats? Why did the ship sink so quickly? Why didn't a nearby ship help? Was it an avoidable tragedy? Read the facts, then decide what to think for yourself.

"I cannot imagine any condition which would cause a ship to founder. I cannot conceive of any vital disaster happening. . . . Modern shipbuilding has gone beyond that."

—*TITANIC*'S CAPTAIN, EDWARD JOHN SMITH, IN 1907, QUOTED BY THE *NEW YORK TIMES* ON APRIL 16, 1912

"The loss of the *Titanic* was due to criminal carelessness in running at full speed through the ice with a new crew, despite the fact that [the captain] had received repeated warnings by wireless of the vast ice field and bergs that lay in his path."

—MAJOR ARTHUR PEUCHEN, FIRST-CLASS PASSENGER, DISCUSSING CAPTAIN SMITH IN AN INTERVIEW WITH THE *TORONTO WORLD* ON APRIL 20, 1912

More here

For key to symbols, see page 112.

Captain Edward John Smith
Carpathia shipwreck
Major Arthur Peuchen

Titanic*: Voices from the Disaster*
by Deborah Hopkinson

***882½ Amazing Answers to Your Questions about the* Titanic**
by Hugh Brewster
and Laurie Coulter

A Night to Remember (1958) is a well-researched film about the boat and the sinking.

***Secrets of the* Titanic** (1986) is a documentary about finding the wreck.

Titanic (2012), a TV miniseries, follows passengers of different classes on board the ship.

Story of a disaster

Titanic's story began when rival shipping companies competed to make money by building the biggest and best ship ever. *Titanic* was White Star's ultimate ship, yet it sank in only a few hours. The discovery of the wreck in 1985 added a fascinating new chapter to this tragic story.

1880

A new start

The Age of Migration began as Europeans escaped famine, poverty, or persecution by moving to the US. They boarded fast new steamships to cross the Atlantic Ocean.

CHEAP FARES ENCOURAGED MILLIONS OF EUROPEAN EMIGRANTS TO SAIL WEST

1907

Rival lines

Cunard was White Star's main rival for US-bound European passengers. Cunard launched the sleek, fast liners *Mauretania* and *Lusitania* on the transatlantic route. White Star decided to compete with even bigger ships.

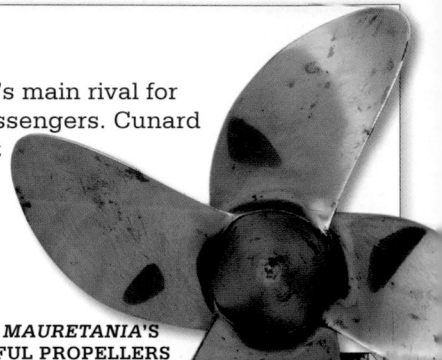

ONE OF *MAURETANIA*'S POWERFUL PROPELLERS

1908

Harland and Wolff put up an enormous steel frame over two new slipways to build the liners Olympic *and* Titanic.

GIANT GANTRY

•1870 1880 • • 1900 •1910

White dots represent 10-year increments.

JAN. 18, 1868

Businessman Thomas Ismay bought the White Star Line, a shipping company that had gone bankrupt.

1869

Irish shipbuilder Harland and Wolff started making ships for White Star.

JULY 1908

White Star's owners agreed on the design for the new ships that were to be built by Harland and Wolff.

MAR. 1909

Titanic*'s keel was laid down at Harland and Wolff's yard number 401.*

OCT. 1910

Riveters finished attaching the huge steel plates that formed Titanic*'s hull.*

1902

American takeover

US banker J. P. Morgan bought White Star for the International Mercantile Marine Co. He wanted to control the transatlantic travel market so that he could raise prices. He provided funds to build new White Star ships.

J. P. MORGAN

Owner, International Mercantile Marine Co.

Lived 1837–1913

Morgan was a powerful and influential businessman who ran railroad and steel companies. He booked a passage on *Titanic* but canceled at the last minute.

MAY 31, 1911

Cheering crowds

Many thousands watched *Titanic* touch water for the first time, at its launch. Ten months of finishing and furnishing began, turning it into a floating palace.

TITANIC'S LAUNCH

APR. 10, 1912

Setting sail

Titanic departed from Southampton. Its passengers included wealthy people who liked to travel on the maiden voyages of luxury liners.

PASSENGERS BOARDING

APR. 16, 1912

Sinking ship

Relatives of *Titanic*'s passengers and crew, desperate for news of survivors, besieged White Star offices. The names were slowly radioed from *Carpathia*, and the world was shocked that so many lives had been lost on an "unsinkable" ship.

CROWDS AWAITING *CARPATHIA*'S ARRIVAL

APR. 14, 1912
Titanic *sailed into the night at full speed, despite warnings of icebergs on the route.*

11:40 PM, APR. 14, 1912
Titanic *hit an iceberg. Few believed the damage was serious, and lifeboats were launched with empty seats.*

ICEBERG!

APR. 18, 1912
Arriving in New York, Carpathia *was met by a crowd of 40,000.*

APR. 19–JULY 3, 1912
US and British authorities both held inquiries.

MAY 31, 2009
Millvina Dean, the last survivor from Titanic, *died. She had sailed on the ship as a two-month-old baby.*

1912 • 10 • • • • • • 17 • 18 • 19 • 1980 • • • • • 2010

White dots represent 1-day increments.

FEB.–APR. 1912
Coal shortages meant that fuel had to be saved for Titanic. *So White Star canceled other voyages and transferred passengers to* Titanic.

2:20 AM, APR. 15, 1912
Titanic *sank. Only one lifeboat returned for survivors. Others feared the weight of more people would sink them, so they stayed away.*

SEPT. 1985
An expedition led by Dr. Robert Ballard discovered remains from Titanic *scattered across the ocean floor, 12,144 ft. (3,701 m) down.*

JULY–SEPT. 1987
An expedition recovered about 1,800 objects from the wreck.

4:10 AM, APR. 15, 1912

Rescue ship

The liner *Carpathia* rescued the first boatload of survivors after a freezing night at sea. Many needed treatment for frostbite.

INJURED RADIO OPERATOR HAROLD BRIDE

JULY 13, 1986

Wreck explored

The submersible *Alvin* explored and photographed the wreck stuck in the sand. The images sparked fresh interest in *Titanic*'s story.

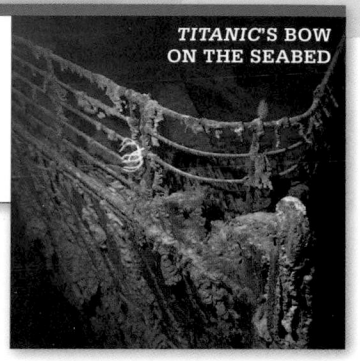

TITANIC'S BOW ON THE SEABED

2,223 people were on *Titanic*; **only 706 survived**

Ship technology

In the late 19th century, the demand for bigger, faster ships spurred the development of transatlantic liners powered by new technologies such as steam turbines and propellers.

Travel to a new land

Millions of people left Europe for new lives in the United States. The only way to reach the US was to sail across the Atlantic Ocean—a long journey at the time.

New cabins

Propellers replaced paddles, freeing up space for more cabins. This area became the quarters for "steerage," or third-class, passengers. Fares were low, but they added up to profits for ship owners.

Sleek or wide?
Some ships were designed with sleek hulls, to slice quickly through the water. Others were built in wider, more stable shapes, to fit extra passengers.

Safe harbor
The large liners could dock only at ports with deep, ice-free harbors.

From sailboats to liners

Ships increased in size to carry more passengers and to hold the coal that was needed to power the new steam engines. To be the biggest and best, liners were beautifully furnished, like luxury hotels.

Paddles
Paddles (right) took up a lot of space and required large quantities of coal to power them.

Propellers
The enormous propellers on the new ships provided more power and used less fuel.

SS *Great Western*

First voyage	1838
Owner	Great Western Steamship
Propulsion	Paddles and sails
Speed	8.5 knots (10 mph / 16 kph)

SS *Great Western*
This oak-hulled boat, powered by a steam-driven paddle, was built for Atlantic trade.

SS *Great Britain*

First voyage	1845
Owner	Great Western Steamship
Propulsion	A propeller and sails
Speed	11 knots (13 mph / 20 kph)

SS *Great Britain*
This was the first iron ocean liner with a propeller.

SS *Teutonic*

First voyage	1889
Owner	White Star
Propulsion	Twin propellers
Speed	20 knots (23 mph / 37 kph)

6-day crossing

1,490 passengers

SS *Teutonic*
This was the first modern liner built especially for passengers.

No more sails
Teutonic *was the first White Star liner without sails.*

SS *Kaiser Wilhelm der Grosse*

First voyage	1897
Owner	Norddeutscher Lloyd
Propulsion	Twin propellers
Speed	22 knots (25 mph / 41 kph)

6-day crossing

1,506 passengers

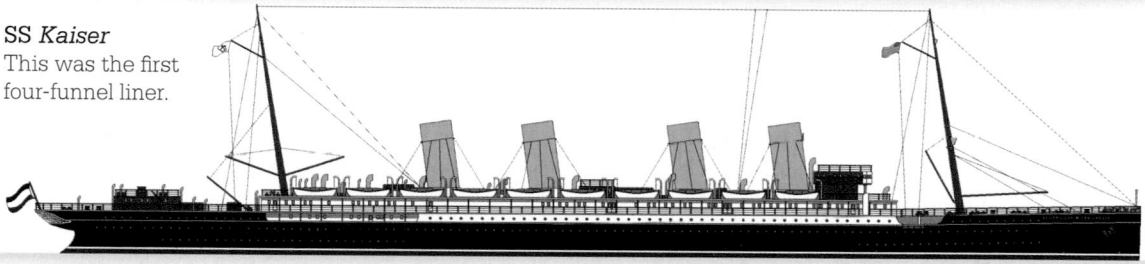

SS *Kaiser*
This was the first four-funnel liner.

RMS *Mauretania*

First voyage	1907
Owner	Cunard
Propulsion	4 propellers
Speed	26 knots (30 mph / 48 kph)

5-day crossing

2,198 passengers

RMS *Mauretania*
This superfast liner offered luxury accommodations.

Titanic's twin sister

RMS *Olympic* was built before *Titanic* was. The shipbuilders copied many features from *Mauretania*. These included elevators, a French-style café, and a grand staircase. *Titanic*'s design had more first-class cabins.

RMS *Olympic*
At the time, this was the world's most luxurious ship.

Safety measure
Watertight compartments helped prevent sinking.

RMS *Titanic*

First voyage	1912
Owner	White Star
Propulsion	3 propellers
Speed	22.5 knots (26 mph / 42 kph)

6-day crossing

2,223 passengers

RMS *Titanic*
Titanic was the world's largest ship when it was built.

Deck windows
Screens on the promenade deck kept out spray.

Transatlantic rivals

Shipping companies White Star and Cunard battled for the ticket money of millions, competing to build the best ships. The race inspired the giant, luxurious *Titanic*.

White Star Line

White Star originally took gold seekers to Australia, but it failed when the gold rush faded. Under Thomas Ismay, it turned its attention to the United States.

1845 The White Star Line was founded in Liverpool, UK.

1868 White Star went bust and was bought by Thomas Ismay.

1869 Ismay hired Harland and Wolff shipyard to build all White Star ships.

1876 The company profited by carrying Royal Mail.

1899 Thomas Ismay died, and his son J. Bruce Ismay took his place.

1902 American J. P. Morgan added White Star to his International Mercantile Marine fleet.

1907 Ismay and Harland and Wolff agreed to build three ships, including *Olympic* and *Titanic*.

WHITE STAR LINE

Luxury liners

With money from US financier J. P. Morgan, J. Bruce Ismay began to develop liners of unparalleled luxury that could compete with Cunard ships. His ships left Southampton for New York every Wednesday.

Why White Star?
Even passengers in third class on a White Star liner were treated well. Families, single women, and married couples were given their own cabins.

Special colors
These ships had "White Star buff" and black funnels.

J. BRUCE ISMAY

Chairman, White Star Line

Lived 1862–1937

Ismay always traveled on his ships' maiden voyages.

[Big shippers]

State of the art

Cunard was the first shipping line to regularly run passenger ships on transatlantic routes. It introduced new technologies such as turbine engines, electricity, and radio. Its ships sailed from Liverpool to New York every Saturday.

Why Cunard?
Cunard's biggest selling point was the speed of its ships. But it also began to match White Star in comfort.

Red livery
All Cunard ships had red and black funnels.

SAMUEL CUNARD
Founder, Cunard Line
Lived 1787–1865
Cunard moved from Canada to Britain to run his company.

New rival

German line Norddeutscher Lloyd (NDL) became a major transatlantic rival in 1897. In that year, it launched *Kaiser Wilhelm der Grosse*, which won the Blue Riband for the fastest ocean crossing.

Power of four
NDL's *Kaiser Wilhelm der Grosse* set a trend with its four funnels.

1840 Samuel Cunard founded the British and North American Royal Mail Steam Packet Company.

1848 The growing fleet started making trips to New York.

1880 The fleet was renamed the Cunard Line, and more ships were built.

1881 Cunard's new all-steel liner, *Servia*, was one of the first ships with full electric lighting.

1902 The British government loaned Cunard money for two superliners.

1903 Hungary agreed to send 30,000 emigrants a year to New York on *Carpathia*.

1907 *Lusitania* joined the fleet, followed by its sister ship *Mauretania*.

Cunard Line

Cunard was named for its founder, Samuel Cunard. He won a contract to carry British mail across the Atlantic. His line also carried emigrants.

CUNARD LINE

PAVILION.

Promenaders

On a promenade—a long, open walkway—people could relax, chat, and show off their finest clothes. In the early 20th century, it was a place to see and be seen. There were promenades in parks, gardens, and seaside towns, such as this one by the coast in Scarborough, in northeast England. They were so popular that ocean liners provided promenade decks so that passengers could take leisurely strolls.

Immigration [Dream ticket]

Between 1836 and 1914, more than 30 million Europeans sailed across the Atlantic Ocean for a fresh start in the United States. They were often escaping famine, poverty, or persecution. Ocean liners such as *Titanic* were crammed with immigrants.

Rising numbers

The peak of the Age of Migration was in 1907, when 1,285,349 Europeans stepped onto US soil for the first time. By then, 15.7 percent of the US population was made up of people who had been born in other countries.

High-rise living
Many Europeans went to cities such as Chicago, Philadelphia, and New York City, where they crammed into tall tenements.

Promise of work

The United States needed people to make clothes, build homes, and farm the western part of the country, which was becoming accessible by rail. There were many opportunities for workers.

Spreading west
Farmland was available to people willing to open up the hostile prairie frontier and grow crops for the increasing population.

Coming to the US
Total immigration figures clearly show the overall rise in numbers of immigrants.

Eyewitness

NAME: Golda Meir

LIVED: 1898–1978

FROM: Russia

DETAILS: Golda Meir's father left his family in Russia in 1903 to travel to the US. It took him three years to save the money for his wife and three daughters to join him. Golda was eight then. She later became prime minister of Israel.

"I can remember only the hustle and bustle of those last weeks in Pinsk. . . . Going to America then was almost like going to the Moon. . . . We were all bound for places about which we knew nothing at all and for a country that was totally strange to us."

UNITED STATES

Ellis Island

70%
of all immigrants entered through New York

Annie Moore
Annie Moore, a 15-year-old from Ireland, and her younger brothers were the first to enter Ellis Island.

Ellis Island

In 1890, the US federal government took control of the rising number of immigrants. A new facility was built on Ellis Island in New York Bay. Third-class passengers were ferried from their ships to Ellis Island to be checked for illnesses and interviewed. About 2 percent were sent back where they had come from.

Mass exodus

The mass exodus from Europe was triggered by many circumstances. Religious or political persecution, lack of food or shelter, and a desire for land were just some of the reasons people left their homelands for the unknown.

Irish emigrants
Around 1.5 million Irish people left for the US in a single decade.

IRELAND

Crop failure
In 1845, Ireland's potatoes—an essential crop—were devastated by blight, leading to famine.

GERMANY

Poverty
In Germany, new factories lowered pay and raised prices, and land was in short supply.

SCANDINAVIA

Seeking new land
Most Scandinavian emigrants were rural workers and wanted land to farm.

RUSSIA

Prejudice
From 1881, Russian Jews were persecuted and massacred. Millions left.

EASTERN EUROPE

Eastern European exodus
Poverty and overpopulation caused the Great Economic Immigration from 1880 onward.

ITALY

Emigration from Italy
A rising population in Italy meant that there was not enough work available.

famine
persecution
poverty

1 First steps
On arrival, passengers disembarked, then underwent medical tests. Those who failed were sent to the hospital.

2 Waiting in line
Then they lined up for hours in the registry room and were questioned about how they would support themselves.

3 The Flag of Faces
Today, four in every ten Americans can trace their ancestors back to the people who passed through Ellis Island.

Iceberg ahead!

Dangers for transatlantic liners included other ships, fog, and ice. Icebergs are hard as rock, sharp as knives, and mostly hidden underwater.

Iceberg Alley

Each spring, powerful currents drag fresh icebergs and sea ice south through a stretch of sea 250 miles (400 km) off the coast of Newfoundland, Canada. The ice moves toward the busy shipping routes of the north Atlantic Ocean, forming an area known as Iceberg Alley.

Collision course
The fatal iceberg glided for more than 1,000 miles (1,600 km) to reach *Titanic*'s path.

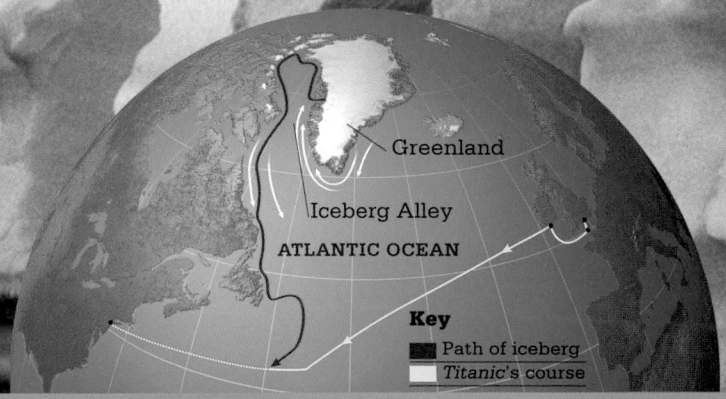

How icebergs form

About 100 glaciers along the coast of Greenland produce the majority of the icebergs that float into the north Atlantic Ocean. Roughly 15,000 icebergs form in that area every year. The iceberg that sank *Titanic* began its existence thousands of years ago, as snowflakes falling across Greenland. Over time, the snow became part of a glacier, which moved slowly toward the sea. Finally, a section calved, or broke off, to form the fatal iceberg.

1 Snowing hard
Snow builds up over thousands of years on high ground. It melts in summer and freezes in winter, forming grainy snow called firn. Fresh snowfall presses the firn down to form solid ice.

2 Glacier
Over the following centuries, layers of ice are crushed into a huge, dense block. This forms a glacier, a giant, slow-moving river of ice. The glacier, pushed by its own weight, moves down toward the sea.

[Snow monster]

Hidden danger

About 85 percent of an iceberg lurks underwater, where its sharp edges do the most damage to ships. Even the section above water is almost impossible to see on a dark night.

Shape changer
Melting and winds constantly change the shapes and sizes of icebergs.

Dark matter
Scattered grit and sections of darker ice can make an iceberg hard to see.

Giant ice cube
Weighing 110,000–220,000 tons on average, icebergs float low in water.

3 Calving
When the glacier reaches the coast, huge sections of ice crash into the ocean. This process, calving, can cause huge waves.

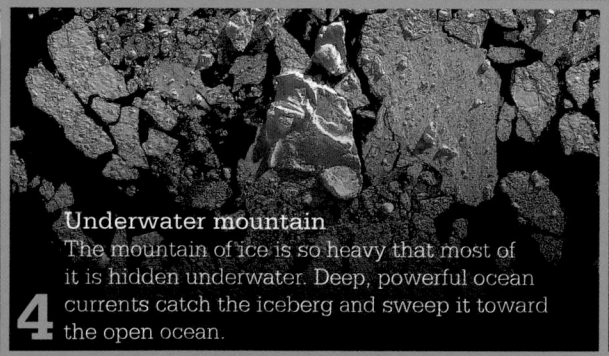

4 Underwater mountain
The mountain of ice is so heavy that most of it is hidden underwater. Deep, powerful ocean currents catch the iceberg and sweep it toward the open ocean.

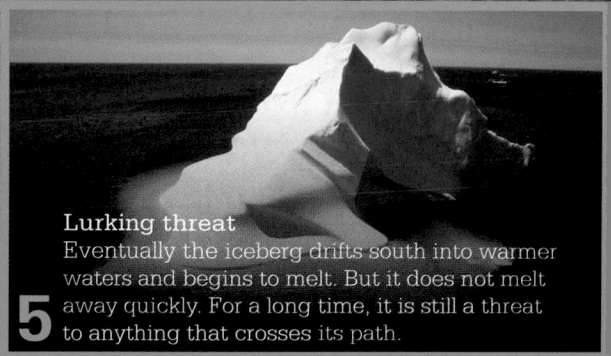

5 Lurking threat
Eventually the iceberg drifts south into warmer waters and begins to melt. But it does not melt away quickly. For a long time, it is still a threat to anything that crosses its path.

Buil
the sh

* Why were *Titanic*'s funnels set at an angle?

* How many giant boilers were built for *Titanic*?

* Where on the ship could passengers cycle?

dling

ip

Shipbuilding [Bigger and better]

The Harland and Wolff site in Belfast, Ireland, was one of the biggest shipyards in the world. Before work could begin on White Star's two new superliners, a gantry, a crane, and two giant slipways had to be built.

Shipyard and port
Titanic was built in Belfast, Ireland, but sailed for the US from Southampton, England.

Gantry
This 220-foot-tall (67 m) metal framework carried 16 mobile cranes.

Titanic
The half-built Titanic *remained on the slipway after its sister ship* Olympic *was launched.*

Eyewitness

NAME: Bram Stoker

DATE: 1907

FROM: Ireland

DETAILS: The author of *Dracula* visited the Harland and Wolff shipyard in 1907. He called it the world's greatest shipbuilding yard.

"No sooner is a vessel launched than preparations begin for laying the keel of another. . . . In the doing of this great work . . . all seems simple, whether it be in perfected details or vast combination. The building of a ship appears to be mere child's play."

Profitable partners

Harland and Wolff had an agreement to design and build all of White Star's ships. Under the contract, the shipbuilder could charge White Star for all the costs of building a ship, plus an extra 5 percent of pure profit.

LORD WILLIAM PIRRIE

Chairman, Harland and Wolff

Lived 1847–1924

Pirrie started work at Harland and Wolff in 1862, as a 15-year-old apprentice. He rose through the ranks and began running the company in 1895. He toured the site each day to check that every job was done properly.

Shift over
In this image, from May 1911, *Titanic* is under construction in the shipyard. To work on *Titanic*, 15,000 men walked to the site from their homes nearby. They worked six-day weeks, with a half-hour lunch each day.

On track
Belfast began running electric trolleys in 1905, thanks to profits from the busy shipyard.

Floating crane

Fitting *Titanic*'s massive boilers and funnels would have been impossible without this 220-ton floating crane. It was shipped in from Germany in 1910.

Lifting power
The new crane, 150 feet (46 m) tall, was berthed between the ship and the dock. It was used to fit the 66-ton, 62-foot-high (19 m) double-walled funnels.

Latticed steel

Counterweight
This exerted the force needed to lift up to 275 tons.

Funnel

Jib
This is the moving arm of the crane.

Hinge
This allowed the jib to tilt.

Complete job

Nearly every structural part of the two ships, as well as many of their fixtures and fittings, was designed and made on-site.

1 Making it
Harland and Wolff had workshops for every part of a ship, from engines and staircases to beds and funnels.

2 Moving it
Heavy goods were transported around the 300-acre (121 ha) site by 50 steam-powered cranes on a network of railroad tracks.

3 Fitting it
When a funnel was lifted into place, it was bolted to the deck with a slight backward tilt—to make the ship look speedy.

Keel to hull [Steel body]

The first step in building the biggest ship in the world was to construct the strongest hull. The keel was the ship's spine, with frames curving up and beams running across. Steel plates covered the structure to create the hull, or outer shell.

Handcrafted

The hull had to be built in stages to make sure the ship was resilient. On March 31, 1909, *Titanic*'s designer laid the first keel plate. A year later, frames and beams were attached. Then plates were fitted onto the frames to form a watertight exterior.

Eyewitness

NAME: Filson Young

DATE: 1911

FROM: County Antrim, Ireland

DETAILS: Writer Filson Young visited Harland and Wolff shipyard in 1911.

"Iron struck upon iron, or steel smitten upon steel, or steel upon iron, or iron upon steel—that and nothing else, day in, day out, year in and year out, a million times a minute."

Gantry
Before work began, a gantry, a huge frame, was built to carry workers and equipment.

Starting March 1909: keel laid
The keel formed the strong base along the length of the ship. Wooden blocks, laid at a slight incline, held the steel sections of keel upright as they were joined together.

Steam crane
A system of cranes, powered by steam, moved heavy parts and equipment.

Keel
The keel was formed from steel beams—4.3 ft. (1.3 m) at their widest points.

April 1910: framework finished
Workers attached 300 curved steel frames to the keel. The frames supported the beams, which ran across the ship and held up each deck.

Rivet

Metal "glue"

Titanic's iron rivets were about 1 inch (2.5 cm) thick and 3 inches (7.5 cm) long. They held the hull's giant plates together.

How a rivet works

A rivet was heated to soften it, pushed through holes in two metal plates, held in place on one side, and hammered flat.

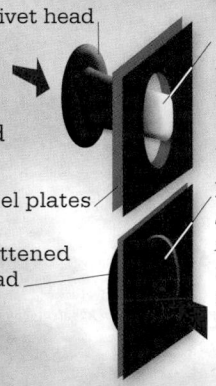

Fitted
A heated rivet fit through two overlapping hull plates.

Hammered
Striking the rivet clamped the plates together.

Teamwork

Four-person teams used long hammers to beat the rivets. They were paid based on how many rivets they fitted, making this competitive work. A record of 12,000 rivets hammered in 1909 was set in 1909.

Smashing time
When riveters stood on scaffolding and beat rivets into place from both sides of the metal hull, the noise was deafening.

3 million rivets held the ship together

Built for strength
The hull extended 97 ft. (29.5 m) in height from the keel to the boat deck.

Framework
Frames were spaced farther apart in the middle of the hull, where there was less stress on the ship.

October 1910: plating finished
The "skin" of the ship was made up of 2,000 riveted steel plates. The largest plates were 36 feet (11 m) long and 6 feet (1.8 m) wide, and weighed 4.2 tons.

Wooden support
Huge timbers supported the hull while it was built.

Plates
Steel plates measured at least 1 in. (2.5 cm) thick.

Mighty hull
The hull covered the biggest ship in the world—882.8 ft. (269 m) long and 92 ft. (28 m) wide.

The workforce

A workforce of thousands toiled six days a week for three years to build *Titanic*. It was noisy and dangerous work—8 men died and 246 were injured.

Line by line
Thomas Andrews, *Titanic*'s designer, oversaw the detailed plans for the ship as they were drawn by hand at the shipyard.

Work and school

About 20 percent of the workforce was unskilled laborers. The skilled laborers carried out the many specialized jobs needed to build a luxury liner; they included young apprentices who were learning trades.

Payday
Each Friday, thousands of workers were paid in cash. Unskilled laborers earned about as much as ship stewards did.

***Titanic* job list**

- *Blacksmith*
- *Boilermaker*
- *Carpenter*
- *Draftsman*
- *Electrician*
- *Engineer*
- *Joiner*
- *Painter*
- *Plumber*
- *Riveter*
- *Sheet metal worker*

THOMAS ANDREWS
Ship designer
Lived 1873–1912

Andrews spent five years learning how to design and build ships at Harland and Wolff. He then became a director at the yard and designed *Titanic*. Andrews headed the guarantee group on *Titanic*—a team of nine shipbuilders who were there to solve problems on the maiden voyage.

Thomas Andrews
Like his uncle Lord William Pirrie (see page 30), who ran the shipyard, Andrews regularly walked around the site to note every detail of the work.

Expert skills

Large, light spaces were built for the draftsmen, who designed and drew plans. Other specialists included carpenters, who built furniture and ship fittings, and blacksmiths, who forged metalwork.

DRAFTSMEN

CARPENTERS

BLACKSMITHS

ng by hand]

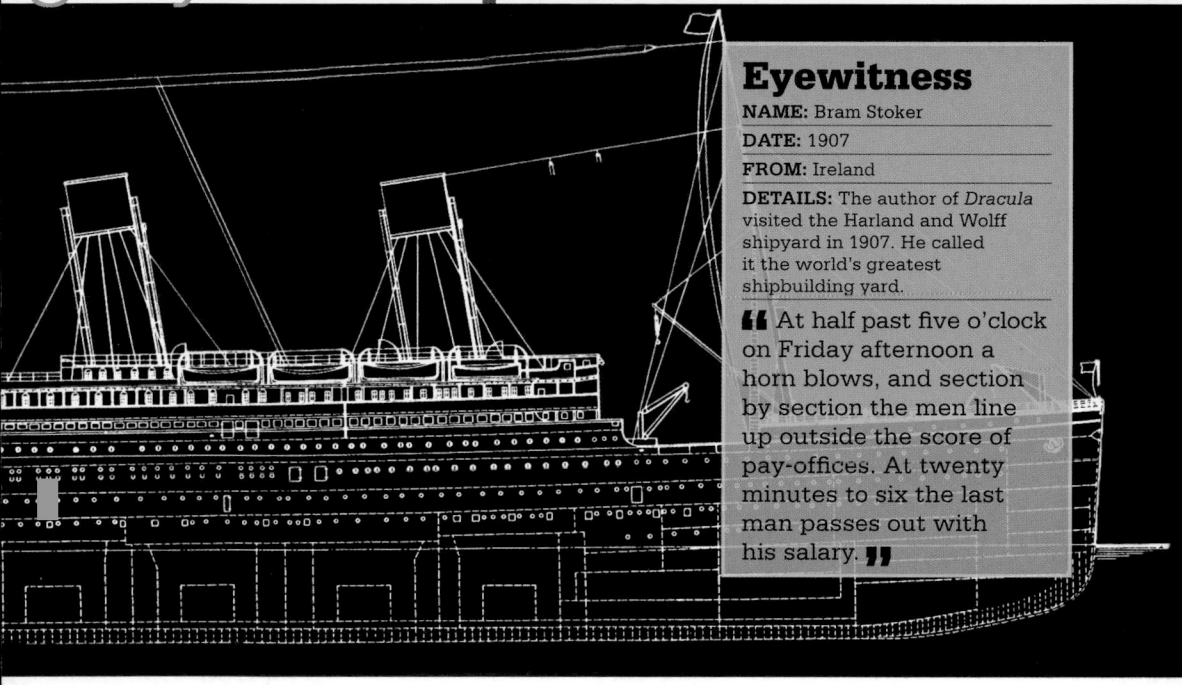

Eyewitness

NAME: Bram Stoker

DATE: 1907

FROM: Ireland

DETAILS: The author of *Dracula* visited the Harland and Wolff shipyard in 1907. He called it the world's greatest shipbuilding yard.

"At half past five o'clock on Friday afternoon a horn blows, and section by section the men line up outside the score of pay-offices. At twenty minutes to six the last man passes out with his salary."

Finest and fines

The very best workers were asked to join the guarantee group, which sailed on maiden voyages. The worst workers faced fines for breaking the many rules, about everything from making tea to stealing.

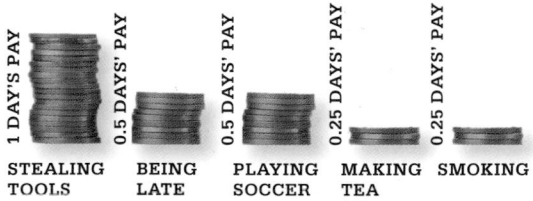

Danger at work

Thousands of men carrying equipment along planks high above the hull spelled danger. Men were injured by falling or by being hit by equipment; one worker was crushed to death at the launch.

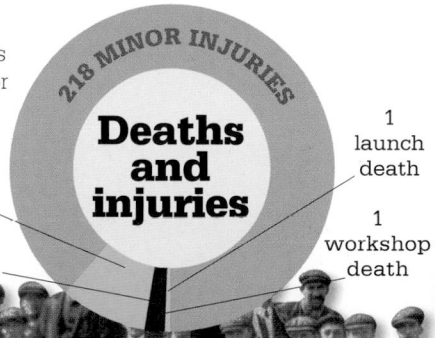

Casualties
Many workers suffered minor injuries, and eight died.

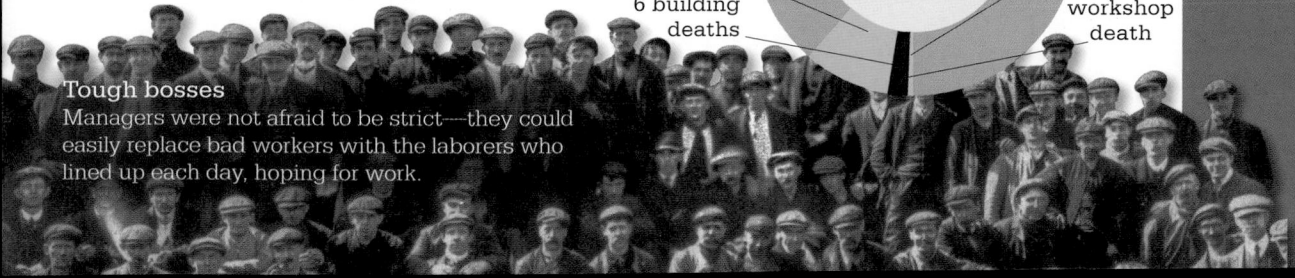

Tough bosses
Managers were not afraid to be strict—they could easily replace bad workers with the laborers who lined up each day, hoping for work.

Young and old
The 15,000 workers included boys as young as 14 years old.

More here

For key to symbols, see page 112

Edward James Harland
Gustav Wilhelm Wolff
Queen's Island, Belfast

"The Last Rose of Summer" and **"Danny Boy"** are typical of the popular Irish songs that were probably sung at the shipyard.

Visit **Titanic Belfast** in Northern Ireland, built on the slipways where the ship itself was built.

See the People's Story exhibition at the **Ulster Folk & Transport Museum** in Northern Ireland to explore the lives of the people who built *Titanic*.

apprentice: a person learning to do skilled labor.

draftsman: a person who draws plans of machinery that will be built.

forge: to heat and hammer metal in order to change its shape.

Powerhouse

The 29 boilers that were needed to power *Titanic* were built by skilled boilermakers in the Harland and Wolff shipyard. Each boiler was the size of a three-story house and contained three or six furnaces to burn the coal that heated water flowing through a network of pipes. The steam that was created powered the engines, generated electricity, supplied the refrigeration plant, and heated the ship's public rooms and the second- and third-class cabins.

Preparations [From hull to hotel]

An army of workers spent ten months transforming *Titanic*'s giant steel hull into a floating palace. Preparations involved everything from laying 200 miles (320 km) of electric cable to screwing in the last brass doorknob.

Out of the water
The ship was propped up in a dry dock while the propellers were fitted and the outside painted. Meanwhile, inside the ship, thousands of workers toiled around the clock to equip and furnish *Titanic*.

Time line: Preparations

April 1911 *Preparations began, with the boilers and engines installed first. For a while,* Titanic *had just three working funnels in place.*

September 20, 1911 Olympic *collided with Royal Navy cruiser* Hawke *and came to Belfast for repairs. This delayed work on* Titanic.

October 11, 1911 *The date of* Titanic*'s maiden voyage, first planned for March 1912, was pushed back to April 1912.*

January 1912 *Sixteen lifeboats were installed on sturdy steel davits on the promenade deck.*

"When the tugs were left behind . . . [*Titanic*] left for Southampton, carrying with her the best wishes of the citizens of Belfast."

—*BELFAST NEWS LETTER*, APRIL 3, 1912

Mainmast
The steel and wood mainmast towered 154 feet (47 m) above A Deck.

Aft crane
The aft cranes primarily loaded food into the refrigerated storerooms.

Paint
A thick coat of oily paint reduced damage from salt water.

February 3, 1912 *The ship was moved to dry dock to fit the propellers and paint the hull. Inside, a Marconi radio was installed.*

March 1912 *The sliding windows on the promenade of A Deck were fitted, one of many alterations made after assessing* Olympic.

March 31, 1912 *The ship was complete. Decorating continued; fresh flowers hid the smell of new paint.*

April 2, 1912 *Five tugs towed* Titanic *out for sea trials. Later that day, it left Belfast for the overnight trip to Southampton.*

Decks 1–5 [Top class]

The officers and first-class passengers could work or relax on the top five decks, far away from the noise and smell of the engines.

A place for everyone

All the classes and most of the crew used the top decks, but they rarely crossed one another's paths. Signs, walls, lockable gates, and separate staircases kept them apart. Strict social divisions were maintained.

Poop deck

Here, third-class travelers could enjoy the views and sea air. Filthy smoke from the funnels drifted over their heads as they walked around the deck.

Café Parisien

Wicker chairs and real ivy plants gave this elegant place the look and feel of a French sidewalk café. It was especially popular with the younger passengers.

Boat layout

- First class
- Second class
- Third class
- Crew

***TITANIC*'S DECKS**

LENGTH: 882.8 FT. (269 M)

Elevator
Second-class passengers had their own elevator.

Second-class dining saloon
This large, oak-paneled room had a grand piano so that diners could enjoy music with their food.

Lifeboats

Docking bridge

Cranes for loading cargo

Two bathrooms for third class

Third-class surgery

Surgery
This room above the hospital was where the doctor saw first- and second-class patients.

Hospital
This had 12 beds. Next to it was a ward with 6 beds, to isolate those with infectious diseases.

Class location

First-class facilities were in the stable middle of the boat, where people were less likely to be seasick.

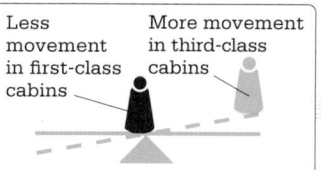

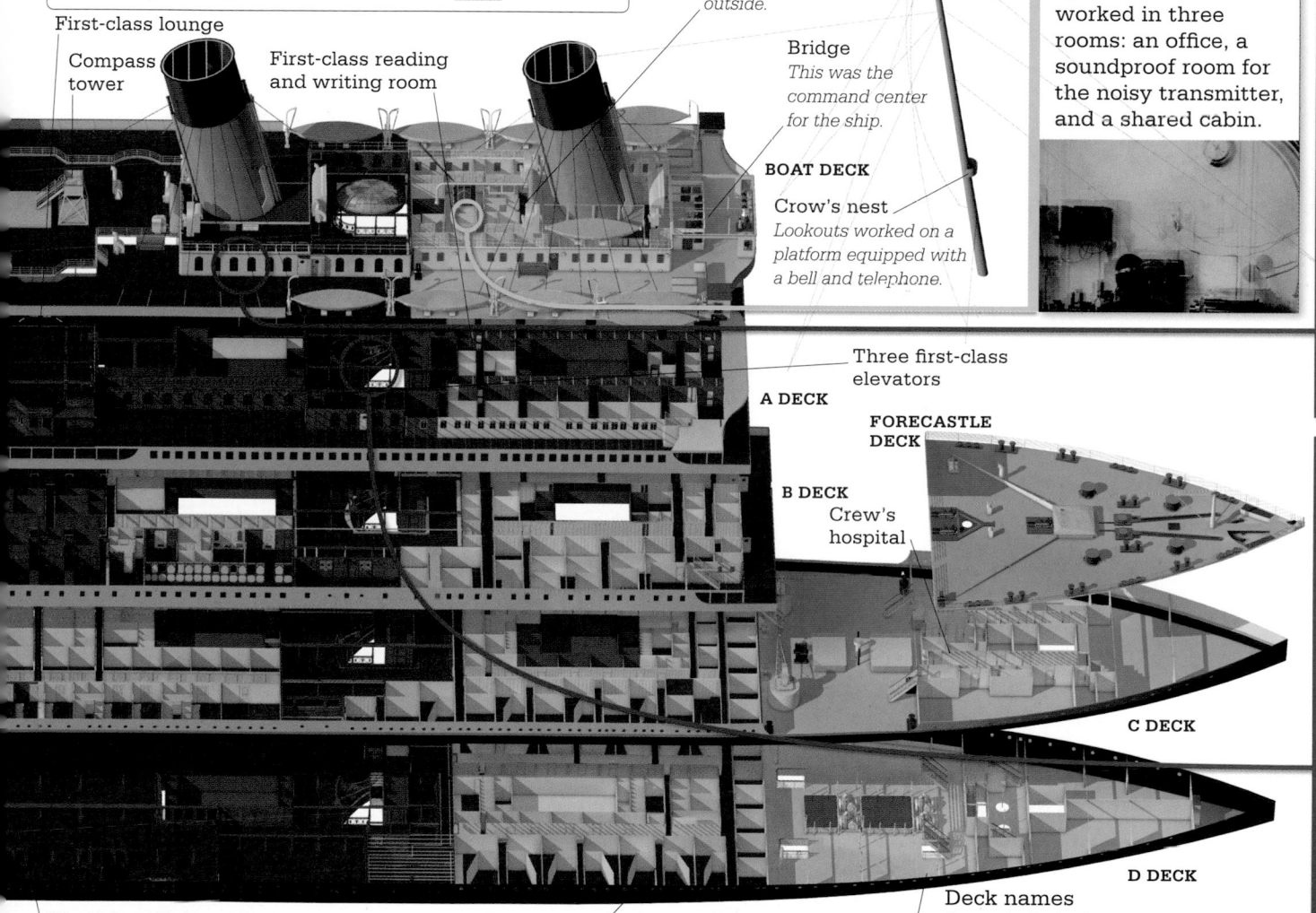

Deck names
Some decks had traditional names. For example, the boat deck got its name because lifeboats were stored there.

Marconi space

The two Marconi radio operators lived and worked in three rooms: an office, a soundproof room for the noisy transmitter, and a shared cabin.

Gym

Gym goers could "race" each other on cycling machines as a large dial showed their speeds. The man here, Lawrence Beesley (see page 54), was in second class but was allowed to try the gym.

Grand staircase

This 60-foot-high (18 m), 16-foot-wide (5 m) staircase rose up through the five decks and was topped by a large chandelier and a giant glass dome.

Decks 6–10 [Powerhouse]

The lower decks housed the workers and the engines that ran the ship. Lower-class passengers and cargo were fit in around them.

Lowest levels

Titanic's lowest row of portholes was on G Deck, just above the waterline. Below was the hot, noisy, and dirty underworld that powered the ship.

***TITANIC*'S DECKS**

Boat layout

- First class
- Second class
- Third class
- Crew
- Storage

Potato storage
This held 40 tons of potatoes, and there was an electric peeling machine next door.

Barber shop

The second-class barbers sold toys, souvenirs, postcards, and pens with the *Titanic* and White Star logos—plus pincushions shaped like life preservers.

Engines

On each side of the ship, an engine ran a propeller. Steam from the engines also ran a central propeller and a turbine. This produced a smooth, efficient journey.

Musicians' rooms
The musicians had a cabin and an instrument room here.

Third-class cabins
Although many cabins were here, their nearest bathrooms were two decks above.

Food storerooms
Chilled rooms stored foods such as fruit, eggs, and ice cream.

Storerooms for groceries, dried fruit, wine, and champagne

Bakery and slaughterhouse

Refrigerated cargo

Rudder
The 101-ton rudder was 79 ft. (24 m) high and 15 ft. (5 m) wide. Seven massive pivoting bolts held it in place.

Propellers
Each outer propeller measured 23 ft. (7 m) across and weighed 38 tons.

Freshwater tanks
Seven tanks like these held a total of 962 tons of drinking water.

Electricity supply
Electricity was generated by four dynamos.

Engine rooms
Each of the two main engines was as tall as a three-story house.

Scotland Road
This passageway was named after a busy street in the port of Liverpool, UK.

Waiters' cabins

Stewards' bathrooms

Shared cabins
These were cheap, sparse cabins for single men.

Third-class dining room

E DECK

F DECK

Squash court

G DECK

Post office

Specie room
Gold and silver coins were secure here, hidden behind luggage.

ORLOP DECK

Ballast tank

TANK TOP

Boiler rooms
There were 24 double-ended boilers and 5 single-ended boilers.

Double bottom
The tank top formed the double bottom of the hull, another safety feature.

Orlop deck
The orlop deck was not a solid deck—it was a platform that the engines rose through.

Decks 6–10
Passengers went only as low as G Deck. Cargo space and the tank top, where the ship's engineers and firemen worked, lay below.

Kennels

Titanic had its own dog kennels. The fare was $10 per animal, plus a butcher's fee for meat scraps. The crew exercised dogs on the poop deck. White Star was also happy to carry cats, birds, and monkeys.

Turkish baths

Visitors to the Turkish baths relaxed in heated steam rooms, then plunged into a cold pool. This was followed by massages called shampoos. The walls were lined with blue and green tiles.

Swimming pool

Titanic was one of the first liners with a pool. It was filled with heated seawater and was popular with passengers, although the water sloshed around as the ship rolled.

Safety [Unsinkable?]

Was *Titanic* safe? It included all the most modern safety features.Crew, passengers, and bystanders alike were convinced that the ship was unsinkable.

Radio for help

Titanic was equipped with a new technology—wireless radio. This had already helped another ship in peril. On January 23, 1909, RMS *Republic* struck another ship and began to sink. Radio distress signals summoned other vessels and lifeboats to ferry 1,700 people to safety.

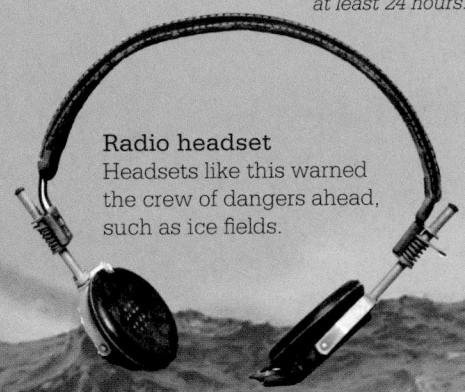

Radio headset
Headsets like this warned the crew of dangers ahead, such as ice fields.

Cork float panels
Cork panels enabled life jackets to float for at least 24 hours.

Plenty of life jackets
Titanic stored 3,560 cork and canvas life jackets all over the ship, in wardrobes and on racks. They did not need to be inflated.

Eyewitness

NAME: Captain John Ranson

DATE: January 1909

FROM: United Kingdom

DETAILS: John Ranson was an experienced captain who commanded White Star ships for many years. He was captain of *Baltic*, one of the ships that heard *Republic*'s distress calls and came to its aid.

"Who would have thought ten years ago of wireless messages to be used in saving life at sea? . . . The passenger on a well-equipped transatlantic liner is safer than he can be anywhere else in the world."

Eyewitness

NAME: Charlotte Collyer

DATE: June 10, 1912

FROM: Basingstoke, UK

DETAILS: Charlotte Collyer boarded *Titanic* with her husband and daughter. Like many others, she thought *Titanic* was the safest of ships.

"There is one impression that will never leave me. It is the irony of the faith that I had in the big ship. 'She is unsinkable,' I had been told, 'she is the safest boat afloat.'"

Unsinkable

White Star's promotional materials highlighted the ship's safety: "These two wonderful vessels [*Olympic* and *Titanic*] are designed to be unsinkable."

Eyewitness

NAME: Karl Behr

DATE: ca. 1912

FROM: New York

DETAILS: Karl Behr was a 26-year-old US tennis star who went to Europe and boarded *Titanic* to follow the woman he wanted to marry.

"To our minds the idea of the *Titanic* sinking was preposterous. . . . We had read about many of the features of this great new ship, of which not the least emphasized was its unsinkability."

Eyewitness

NAME: *New York Times*

DATE: October 1910

FROM: United States

DETAILS: The *New York Times* ran an article on *Olympic*, *Titanic*'s sister ship. The paper was impressed by the ship's safety features.

"So complete will be the system of safeguarding devices on board this latest of ocean giants that . . . it is claimed that she will be practically unsinkable and absolutely unburnable."

Watertight compartments

There were 15 watertight doors that could be closed from the bridge of the ship. These created 16 watertight compartments along the bottom half of the ship. The ship could stay afloat even if 4 of these compartments flooded.

Mabel Francatelli's life jacket

This canvas life jacket belonged to one of *Titanic*'s survivors, Mabel Francatelli, who was 30 years old at the time of the sinking. She was secretary to Lady Duff Gordon (see pages 50–51) and came from London. The life jacket carries her faded signature as well as the signatures of seven other survivors.

Safely secured

A jacket was put on over the head and secured with fabric ties.

More than enough lifeboats

Board of Trade regulations said that ships that weighed more than 10,000 tons—*Titanic* was 51,000 tons—should carry 16 lifeboats. *Titanic* had 20.

Lifeboats

Titanic carried 16 wooden boats and 4 canvas "collapsibles."

Eyewitness

NAME: Sir Alfred Chalmers

DATE: 1912

FROM: British Board of Trade

DETAILS: Sir Alfred Chalmers was nautical adviser to the British Board of Trade from 1896 to 1911. He decided that large liners did not need more lifeboats, because they were so safe. At the British inquiry after *Titanic*'s sinking, he explained his reasoning

"I found [that ships were] the safest mode of travel in the world. . . . [16 lifeboats] was the maximum number that could be rapidly dealt with at sea and that could be safely housed.
. . . If you went on crowding the ships with boats you would require a crew . . . which would be carried uselessly across the ocean, that never would be required to man the boats."

Eyewitness

NAME: Unnamed journalist

DATE: June 1911

FROM: *Shipbuilder* magazine

DETAILS: This magazine ran stories about how ships were made. In 1911, it devoted a whole issue to *Titanic* and its sister ship *Olympic*, including this description of the watertight compartments.

"In the event of an accident, or at any time when it may be considered advisable, [the] captain can, simply by moving an electric switch, instantly close the emergency doors . . . and make the vessel practically unsinkable."

The voy

* Who added glamour at Cherbourg?

* What new invention was carried as cargo?

* How was the grand staircase lit up?

---

age

Setting off [All aboard]

On the morning of Wednesday, April 10, 1912, passengers boarded the towering *Titanic* for its maiden voyage. At Southampton, the new crew struggled to direct people to their cabins, through a maze of corridors filled with vases of flowers to disguise the smell of fresh paint.

First-class view
From the moment passengers arrived to board *Titanic*, they were divided by their ticket class. First-class passengers boarded at the highest level, and third class at the lowest gangway.

Welcome to *Titanic*

First-class passengers were welcomed aboard by officers or the captain. Those in third class had quick medical inspections to make sure that they were healthy and would be allowed into the United States.

Passengers on and off
Passengers could board at several ports, and some did not travel all the way to the US. At Cherbourg, France, 24 people got off *Titanic*, and 7 left at Queenstown, Ireland.

Eyewitness

NAME: Charles Lightoller

LIVED: 1874–1952

FROM: Hampshire, UK

DETAILS: Lightoller was second officer on *Titanic*. He was going to be first officer but was replaced by William Murdoch, who was transferred to *Titanic* at the last minute.

"At last sailing day arrived, and from end to end the ship, which for days had been like a nest of bees, now resembled a hive about to swarm. As 'zero' hour drew near, so order could be seen arriving out of chaos. On the stroke of the hour, the gangway was lowered, the whistle blew, ropes were let go, and the tugs took the strain."

Last stop

At Queenstown, a fleet of boats ferried sellers of Irish lace, linen, and woolens to *Titanic*. American millionaire John Jacob Astor IV bought plenty of finery from the vendors for his new wife, Madeleine.

First ports of call
Titanic crossed to France and Ireland for more passengers and mail before heading west.

First-class service

There were two special boat trains from London to Southampton. One was reserved for first-class passengers, who were escorted by White Star staff.

Margaret Brown

Brown was a wealthy American who had met the Astors on their honeymoon in Egypt. When Brown heard that her grandson was very ill, she decided to travel home with the famous couple, and they boarded at Cherbourg.

First class [Millionaire style]

For passengers in first class, *Titanic* was a luxurious hotel run by an army of stewards. First-class cabins were in the stable middle of the ship, where passengers were less likely to be seasick.

The rich list

There were many millionaires on board, as well as other aristocratic and wealthy first-class passengers. Some were traveling on business. Many rich Americans were returning home from vacations in Europe.

Service

There were 225 stewards to serve 329 first-class passengers. They were on call all day until late evening.

Electricity

Several first-class luxuries were powered by electricity. Most people did not have electricity at home at this time.

Keeping fit
Instructor Thomas McCawley loved to show off his gym.

Electric steam bath
The electric bath, a box heated by lamps, was a fashionable way to relax.

Cabins

The cabins ranged from comfortable single berths to magnificent parlor suites (see pages 52–53).

Louis XVI stateroom
Among the luxurious fittings were silk wall panels, a stained-glass window, and a chaise longue.

First-class couple
Sir Cosmo Duff Gordon, a member of the British aristocracy, was a Scottish landowner and sportsman who had fenced at the 1908 Olympics. He was traveling with his wife, Lucy.

Electrical luxuries

- *Heaters*
- *Table fans*
- *Telephones*
- *Dimmable lamps*
- *Hot running water*
- *Doorbells*

Cabin contents

- *Wood sprung bed with hair mattress*
- *Chaise longue*
- *Wardrobe*
- *Dressing table*
- *Washbasin*
- *Carpeted floor*

1 member of staff served 1.5 first-class passengers

Eyewitness

NAME: Lucy Christiana, Lady Duff Gordon

LIVED: 1863–1935

FROM: London, UK

DETAILS: Lady Duff Gordon was an upscale dress designer with salons in London, Paris, and New York.

"Like everyone else I was entranced by the beauty of the liner. I had never dreamed of sailing in such luxury. . . . My pretty little cabin, with its electric heater and pink curtains, delighted me, so that it was a pleasure to go to bed. Everything about this lovely ship reassured me."

First-class facilities

Deck areas: promenade deck, plus two private promenades

Lounge

Reading and writing room (for ladies only)

Smoking room (for gentlemen only)

Gymnasium and squash court

Turkish bath and heated swimming pool

Dining room, à la carte restaurant, and two cafés

Barbershop

Grand staircase and three elevators

Cost of most expensive suite: $4,350 (equivalent to $87,000 today)

The smoking room

A real fireplace, leather chairs, stained-glass windows, and wood-paneled walls inlaid with mother-of-pearl made the first-class smoking room—for gentlemen only—the grandest room on the liner. This picture is of the smoking room on *Titanic*'s sister ship *Olympic*.

Eyewitness

NAME: Ida Straus

LIVED: 1849–1912

FROM: Germany; Straus's family immigrated to the US when she was five.

DETAILS: Straus was married to Isidor Straus, one of the owners of Macy's department store in New York. They were returning to the US from a European vacation and were transferred to *Titanic* after their trip on another ship was canceled due to a coal strike.

"What a ship! So huge and so magnificently appointed. Our rooms are furnished in the best of taste and most luxuriously, and they are really rooms, not cabins."

First-class berths

The design of each first-class cabin was chosen from 11 different historical eras. This stateroom, Cabin B-59, had dark oak panels and a canopy bed in the "Old Dutch" style. The doors led to the family rooms in the suite.

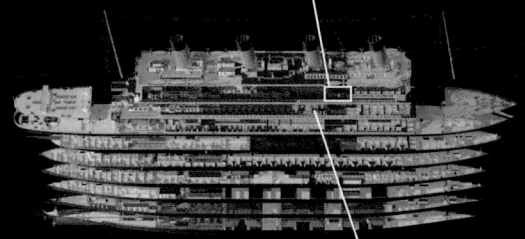

Heater
First-class cabins and bathrooms had electric heaters.

First-class passenger
American Benjamin Guggenheim boarded the ship at Cherbourg with his valet, Victor Giglio, and a friend, Léontine Aubart. He and Giglio were in stateroom B-84. His chauffeur, René Pernot, traveled in second class.

Second class

Second class on *Titanic* was as good as first class on most other liners. Passengers had their own staircase, though it was less grand than the one for first class.

"Loto" and "Louis"
These young French boys were rarely far from their father (see page 104).

Eyewitness

NAME: Lawrence Beesley
LIVED: 1877–1967
FROM: London, UK
DETAILS: Beesley was a science teacher visiting his brother in Canada.

"The ship is like a palace. There is an uninterrupted deck run of 165 yards [150 m] for exercise and a ripping [great] swimming-bath. . . . My cabin is ripping, hot and cold water and a very comfy-looking bed and plenty of room."

Service

There were 76 stewards on hand to serve the 285 second-class passengers. Among their jobs was changing bedsheets every day.

Library steward
One steward was in charge of the second-class library.

In the middle

Second-class passengers included teachers, priests, families, servants, and a band of eight musicians. Also among them was Joseph Laroche, the only black passenger on the liner.

Reading encouraged
Children could enjoy books borrowed from the second-class library on C Deck.

Cabins

These were comfortable, but the beds were attached to the walls, and the floors were tiled, not carpeted.

Bunking up
Many second-class cabins had space-saving bunk beds.

Cabin contents

- *Beds*
- *Full set of linens*
- *Wardrobe*
- *Small settee*
- *Washbasin*
- *Chamber pot*
- *Single lightbulb, no shade*
- *Linoleum-tiled floor*

Stuart Collett
Sidney Clarence Stuart Collett was a 25-year-old student training to be a minister like his father. He had paid $50 (equivalent to $1,000 today) to emigrate and join the rest of his family in Port Byron, NY.

[Second best?]

Second-class facilities

Deck area: boat deck	
Dining room for shared meals	
Smoking room	
Library (lounge)	
Barbershop	
Shared bedrooms	
Staircase	
Elevator	
Cost of average fare:	*$66 (equivalent to $1,320 today)*

Eyewitness

NAME: Eva Hart

LIVED: 1905–1996

FROM: London, UK

DETAILS: Hart was seven years old when her family immigrated to Canada. Their first voyage was canceled because of a coal strike, so they switched to *Titanic*.

"My father was delighted when they offered him a second-class passage in the *Titanic*. The whole world was talking about the *Titanic*. . . . I was seven, I had never seen a ship before. . . . It looked very big. . . . My father was so excited about it and my mother was so upset."

1 member of staff served 3.75 second-class passengers

Well read and well fed
The second-class library was also known as the lounge. It served as a sitting area where passengers took afternoon tea at 4 PM.

Third class [Better fare]

For many third-class passengers, a ticket on *Titanic* provided much better accommodations than they were used to at home. But they were kept away from first-class areas.

Good grub
The food provided was basic, but healthy and plentiful. It included porridge, beef with gravy, and stewed fruit.

Third-class travelers

Many were families or single men fleeing from persecution or poverty in their homelands. They trekked for many weeks to reach Southampton from eastern Europe or Scandinavia. *Titanic* was the next stage in a journey to a new life.

Service

There were 51 stewards, including an interpreter to communicate with the many non-English speakers.

Cabin contents

- *Bunk beds (wood or iron)*
- *Mattresses, pillows, and blankets (no sheets)*
- *Hooks for hanging clothes*
- *Washbasins (some cabins only)*

Food for all

Third-class passengers were served three meals a day in two separate sittings. Women and children also received chicken broth or beef tea at 11 AM—possibly to help fight seasickness.

Dining hall
Long tables were bolted to the floor to keep them from sliding.

Worldly goods
For many, everything they owned was on the ship.

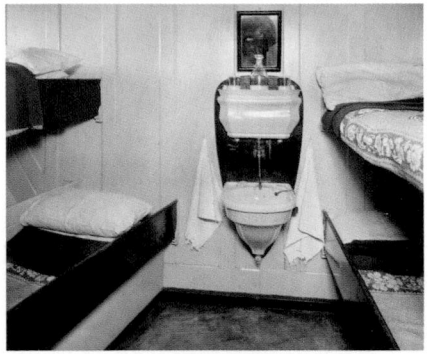

Cabins

Cabins for women and families were toward the back of the boat. Single men were at the front.

Four-berth cabin
Most cabins had four or six berths.

Crockery
Plates and cups were plain white with the White Star logo.

Third-class general room
This large room allowed groups of third-class passengers to gather and chat, sing, dance, or play games. Nearby was a smoking room with a bar for the men to use.

1 member of staff served 14 third-class passengers

Third-class facilities

Two dining rooms	
Smoking room (for men only)	
General room with bare wooden furniture	
Use of poop deck at the stern	
Stairs	
Two bathtubs, one for each sex	
Cost of lowest single fare:	*$15 (equivalent to $300 today)*

Eyewitness

NAME: Elin Hakkarainen

LIVED: 1888–1957

FROM: Quincy, MA

DETAILS: Hakkarainen had been born in the US but moved away to be with her Finnish husband. They were leaving Finland to avoid his conscription into the Russian army. They switched their passage from *Mauretania* to *Titanic* and enjoyed the superior standard of its third-class facilities.

"Although we were booked as third class, we still enjoyed many 'extras' on board and had quite a time in our little group. After a couple of days at sea we settled into a routine: attending church services after breakfast, strolling the decks, and during the evening playing games in the third-class general room."

The Goodwin family
Laborer Frederick Goodwin left London to work at a power station in Niagara Falls, NY. From left to right: William, 11; Frederick, 42; Charles, 14; Lillian, 16; Augusta, 43; and Jessie, 10. At the front is Harold, 9. Frederick and Augusta's 19-month-old son, Sidney, is not shown.

Deck to deck

A walk down *Titanic*'s many staircases took passengers and crew from cool first-class luxury to plain third-class rooms to volcano-like heat from furnaces in the ship's depths.

Many layers

This artist's impression shows how *Titanic* was put together like a ten-layer jigsaw puzzle. The corridors and cabins fit neatly around big spaces such as the grand staircase, the dining rooms, and the swimming pool.

Letting in the light

During the day, the grand staircase was illuminated by a huge glass dome that allowed the Sun's rays to flow down many stories. The oval dome was 26 feet (8 m) across. The chandelier in its center had 50 lights that lit the staircase in the evenings.

Linking and lighting
Two massive staircases, plus many smaller flights, linked the decks, allowing everyone to move around easily. It took 10,000 lightbulbs to light all the rooms, from the tiniest storeroom to the most palatial dining room.

Mail room

There were five postal clerks in the mail room. At 48, John Starr March was the oldest of the three American clerks.

Chart room
Here, officers calculated where the ship was and how far it had traveled.

Smoking room
First-class men enjoyed their cigars here.

Enquiry office
Passengers came here to send messages and report problems.

Print room
The crew printed daily menus and news for the passengers.

Third-class bakery
This was one of two bakeries on Titanic *that made bread and pastries.*

Swimming pool
Men could use the pool 6–9 AM and 2–7 PM. Women could use it 9 AM–2 PM.

Post office
Mail was taken here to be sorted. Then it was stored in mailbags to await arrival in New York.

Watertight compartment

Double hull

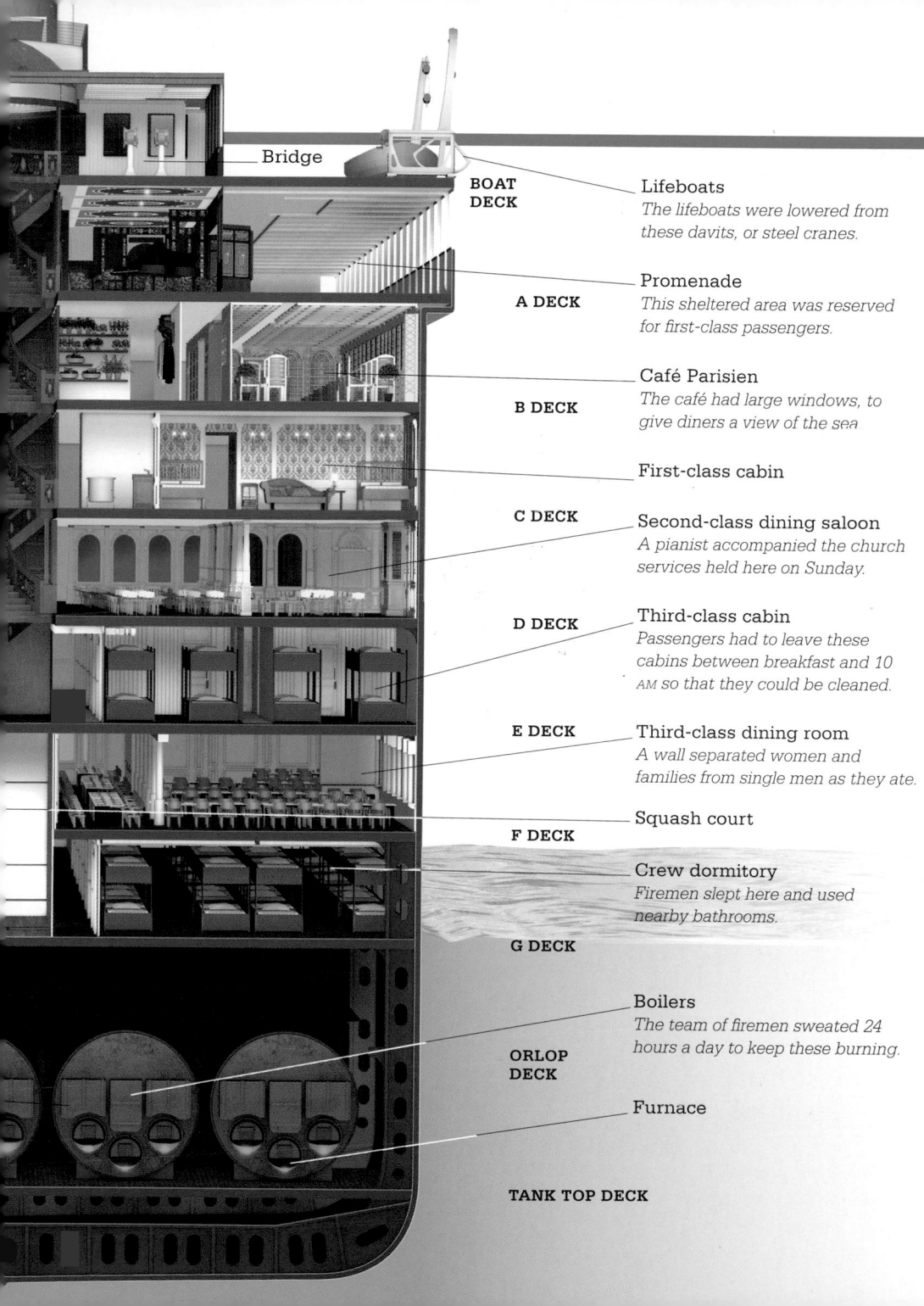

Fine dining

This exclusive restaurant was open from 8 AM to 11 PM. It served first-class diners such as John Jacob Astor IV, the richest man in the US, and his wife Madeleine (left).

Eyewitness

NAME: Eileen Lenox-Conyngham

LIVED: 1900–1993

FROM: Edinburgh, Scotland

DETAILS: At age 11, Lenox-Conyngham sailed on *Titanic* as far as Cherbourg, France. She and her mother, aunt, and younger brother Denis left the ship there.

"We were absolutely staggered by the beauty and size of this great ship. . . . The pride of [the] White Star Line was elegant beyond description."

Third class

Jack Prideaux, age 23, was a steward to *Titanic*'s third-class passengers. Serving third class was not a steward's favorite job—he was less likely to get tips from the poorer passengers.

Crew [Many hands]

Titanic's 899 crew members were ranked in a social order, like the passengers were. Officers were at the top, and stewards were in the middle. At the bottom, both in rank and in location, working in the furnaces, were the stokers.

Popular captain
Officers liked Edward Smith, and wealthy passengers chose to sail on his ships.

In command

The job of commanding the ship was reserved for the captain and the chief, first, and second officers. Junior officers navigated, marked the ship's charts, and checked air and water temperatures.

Hugh McElroy *Chief purser* · James Moody *Sixth officer* · Charles Lightoller *Second officer* · Henry Wilde *Chief officer* · Herbert Pitman *Third officer* · Edward Smith *Captain* · William Murdoch *First officer* · Harold Lowe *Fifth officer* · Joseph Boxhall *Fourth officer*

New ranks
Henry Wilde joined *Titanic* as chief officer at the last minute. Each of the other officers had to move down a rank.

EDWARD JOHN SMITH
Captain

Lived	1850–1912

Smith left school when he was 13 years old to go to sea; he joined White Star in 1880 as a junior officer. Known as "E.J.," he became the world's highest-paid seaman. Starting in 1904, he commanded all White Star maiden voyages. Smith had planned to retire after his trip on *Titanic*.

Only 56 of the 899 crew members were sailors

Working for tips

Stewards made sure that all the passengers were comfortable: They served food and drinks and cleaned rooms. Stewards hoped for tips to add to their weekly pay of $4.50—equivalent to $90 today.

Chief purser
Hugh McElroy was in charge of the stewards and ran the enquiry office. Only the captain and the chief purser dined regularly with the passengers.

Eyewitness

NAME: George Kemish

LIVED: 1888–1912

FROM: Southampton, UK

DETAILS: Kemish, known as "Scooch," earned $30 a month—equivalent to $600 today—to stoke the furnaces. Stokers enjoyed *Titanic*'s new, cleaner conditions.

"Being a new ship on her maiden voyage . . . she was a good job in the stokeholds (not what we were accustomed to in other old ships—slogging our guts out and nearly roasted with the heat)."

Black gang
Workers in the black gang had the filthy job of fetching and shoveling black coal in the hot, noisy furnaces.

Machine men

Engineers, stokers, trimmers, and greasers kept the ship's machinery running. The men worked in teams, in shifts of four hours on, eight hours off. The members of each team shared a dormitory so that they did not disturb others when they finished their shifts.

A variety of work

There were many jobs on the ship, including specialized radio and postal work. Some crew members were employed by other companies and were regarded as rivals for tips or envied for the privileges they enjoyed.

Musicians
Eight independent musicians played in restaurants and public areas and slept in second class.

Postal clerks
Five postal clerks sorted *Titanic*'s mail freight for the US or British mail services.

Cooks
Luigi Gatti's 66 staff members ran the à la carte dining for first class.

Radio men
Two radio operators, employees of Marconi, sent messages for passengers.

Cargo [Loading up]

When *Titanic* reached Ireland, it collected the last of its passengers. It was also loaded with mailbags. Then it finally set out across the Atlantic toward the United States.

Food mountain

The ship had to carry enough supplies for 17 days. There was enough food for the 7,000 meals served daily to passengers and crew.

Fresh supplies

Fresh meat	*75,000 lb. (34,000 kg)*
Butter	*6,000 lb. (2,700 kg)*
Eggs	*40,000*
Sugar	*10,000 lb. (4,500 kg)*
Oranges	*36,000*
Grapes	*1,000 lb. (450 kg)*
Lettuce	*7,000 heads*
Peas	*1.25 tons*
Tomatoes	*2.75 tons*
Potatoes	*40 tons*

APPLES: 36,000

FLOUR: 200 BARRELS

ASPARAGUS: 800 BUNDLES

Boarding and landing
The ship was too big for the harbor in Queenstown, so the passengers were ferried out. A new delivery of 194 mailbags was taken to the mail room. There, more than 3,000 bags of mail and 700 packages were already stacked.

***Titanic* carried**
440 gallons (1,665 L) of ice cream

Steaming!

Titanic carried 5,892 tons of coal, stored in bunkers near the bottom of the ship. A small army of workers called trimmers wheeled and shoveled up to 825 tons every 24 hours to fire the 29 boilers.

***Titanic* carried**
11,000 lb. (5,000 kg) of fresh fish

COAL

Thirsty work
In addition to tankfuls of freshwater, *Titanic* carried 1,500 gallons of fresh milk and 20,000 bottles of beer.

Cargo ship

Titanic had 560 tons of cargo on board, plus passenger baggage. Everything had to be placed carefully along the length of the hold, so that uneven weight would not tip the ship, and all of it would be kept secure and dry.

Personal transport
Passenger William Carter brought a Renault car on board in a wooden crate.

High fashion
Titanic carried 12 cases of ostrich feathers, for adding to fashionable clothes in the US.

Gramophones
A case of some of the newest music players, called Edison gramophones, was on board.

A day on *Titanic*

Titanic was full of activity from early morning until midnight. The crew worked 24 hours a day to serve passengers and sail the ship. Passengers of different classes could not share activities except by special invitation.

Busy days

Passengers were given schedules of mealtimes and other activities. First-class passengers had the most options, but everyone was told when to go to bed.

Crew's day

Most crew members worked for four hours, then rested for eight. Stewards were on call nearly all the time. Waiters worked before, during, and after each meal, so a waiter in first class would be on duty for breakfast from 7 to 11 AM.

Midday mileage

Before lunch, officers posted charts to show where *Titanic* had sailed in the past 24 hours. They were proud of how fast the ship could sail.

Shared shifts
The purser and the captain worked the same shifts that most of the crew did.

Titanic postcard
Postcards of the ship could be bought and mailed to friends back home.

Rooms

Each class had public rooms where passengers could relax. They ranged from very basic to luxurious.

First-class lounge
Along with this comfortable lounge, first class had a smoking room for men and a writing room for women.

Second-class lounge
Also known as the library, this room was mainly for women. Men were more likely to use the smoking room.

Third-class general room
This room and the men's smoking room next door had plain wooden benches and chairs without fabric, so they were easy to clean. Both were for third-class passengers.

The captain toured the ship at 10:30 every morning

Wish you were here

Everyone could send letters home. Radio messages, called marconigrams, were charged by the word, and about 60 were sent per day.

[Hours of fun]

Food

All passengers ate high-quality food, but first class had a choice of restaurants.

Top class
First class had two dining rooms, plus cafés. Elegant dishes included caviar and éclairs.

- 8–10 AM Breakfast
- 1–2:30 PM Lunch
- 4 PM Tea
- 7–9 PM Formal dinner

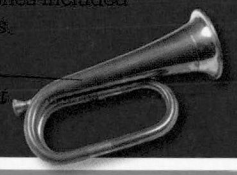

Call to dine
A bugler played at lunch and dinner.

PLATE OF OYSTERS

Come and eat
A gong announced mealtimes. Three-course dinners included a choice of main course, such as curry or fish.

- 8–10 AM Breakfast
- 12:30 PM Lunch
- 4 PM Tea
- 6:30 PM Dinner

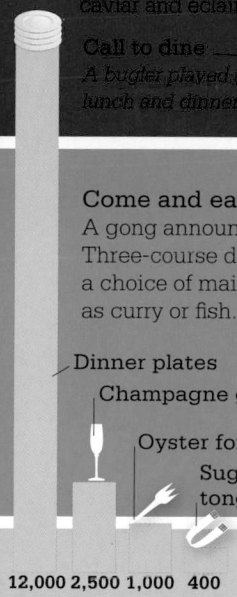

***Titanic* tableware**
Plates had different designs in each class. First class's were decorated in gold, second's in blue and white, and third's with the White Star logo.

How far?
Each day's mileage was a subject of discussion.

Healthy food
The last three-course meal, eaten at 1 PM on April 14, was soup, fresh bread, roast beef, and dessert.

- 8–9 AM Breakfast
- 11 AM Broth for women and children
- 1 PM Dinner
- 6 PM Tea

Broth snack
Chicken broth and beef tea may have helped ease seasickness.

Special cups
Titanic *had 3,000 broth cups with its company logo.*

Entertainment

Each class had a section of deck to stroll along. Activities on *Titanic* ranged from deck games to music.

Sports
First-class passengers could swim, play squash, or use the fitness room.

SWIMMING

CYCLING

SQUASH

Tunes
Passengers could listen to the band or play a piano.

GRAND PIANO

Good night!
Lights in the public rooms were switched off to tell passengers to go to bed.

Lights-out

12:00 AM

Read, write, or play?
Second-class passengers could stroll on the deck or spend the journey reading, writing, or playing games.

On deck
Deck games such as shuffleboard and quoits were popular.

Lounge
The lounge had a library, and tables for card games.

Quoits
Players threw rope rings at a target.

Library
The library even had its own steward.

12:00 AM

Noisy neighbors
The music and dancing in third class could get very noisy—it sometimes disturbed people trying to sleep in nearby cabins.

Variety show
Passengers played their own small instruments, like this accordion, which were easily carried and stored.

10:00 PM

10:30 PM

Child's play

Titanic was a giant playground for children, with deck games such as shuffleboard, and a swing on A Deck. Here, six-year-old Douglas Spedden tries out a spinning top on the first-class promenade, watched by his father, Frederic. The Speddens were traveling back to New York after a family vacation in Europe. They survived the sinking, as did Douglas's nanny, Elizabeth Burns.

Navigation [Where are we?]

Today's satellite technology makes it easy to know where you are when you are at sea. But *Titanic*'s crew members had to use tools such as compasses and sextants, and books of complicated tables of the positions of the stars. They relied on lookouts and radio messages to warn them about obstacles.

Latitude and longitude

A ship's location was fixed, or determined, by finding its latitude and longitude. At least two officers, working as a team, took fixes in the mornings and evenings. Between fixes, they used a system called dead reckoning: They estimated the position of the ship based on its speed and direction.

Radio warnings
Radio messages received through these wires warned of icebergs.

Crow's nest
From here, a lookout kept watch for ice ahead.

Navigator
An officer standing on the deck needed sharp eyesight to read a sextant accurately in dim light.

Lines of latitude
These lines show distance north or south of the Equator.

Lines of longitude
These lines show distance east or west of an imaginary north–south line called the prime meridian.

Navigation tools

In order to determine latitude and longitude, speed, and direction, *Titanic*'s navigators needed certain tools. They used a sextant to fix their position, a taffrail log to check speed, a compass to determine direction, and a chronometer to establish longitude. When they had gathered all this information, officers could plot the ship's course on a chart.

Keeping track
The crew plotted the direction of travel on charts.

Rotator
This was towed through the water, turning to match the ship's speed.

Reading unit
This was usually attached to the taffrail, the rail at the stern of the ship.

Compass
Titanic's iron hull affected its magnetic field, so its four compasses were mounted on nonmagnetic materials such as wood and brass.

Taffrail log
A rotator (top) was attached by a long, stiff line to a reading unit (above) and towed through the water from the stern. The distance traveled was shown on the dial.

Navigating through ice fields

Large ice fields were not a danger often faced by ships on *Titanic*'s route. Ships radioed warnings to one another if they spotted ice, and lookouts scanned the horizon for icebergs. If it was surrounded by icebergs, a ship might stop for the night.

BINOCULARS

Keeping watch
To spot ice, a team of six lookouts on Titanic *looked for reflected light, dark shapes, and the white foam of waves breaking on icebergs.*

? What went wrong?

Could *Titanic* have avoided the iceberg? Experts disagree. What do you think? The lookouts' binoculars had been misplaced. But it was a dark, almost moonless night, so it was difficult to see, and the sea was calm, so no waves broke against the iceberg.

"Anyone with experience of ice at sea knows that those very conditions . . . only rendered the detection of icebergs all the more difficult."

—OFFICER CHARLES LIGHTOLLER, IN A BBC INTERVIEW, 1936

"We could have seen [the iceberg] a bit sooner."

—LOOKOUT FREDERICK FLEET, AT THE US INQUIRY, STATING WHAT MIGHT HAVE HAPPENED IF HE HAD HAD BINOCULARS

Ice warnings sent by other ships did not warn *Titanic*'s officers of ice directly ahead, so the ship continued to sail at high speed.

Sextant
A sextant was used to measure the angle between the Sun, or certain stars, and the horizon. Taking a reading allowed officers to draw a position line along which the ship was traveling. Repeating this three times gave them an accurate position.

Horizon mirror
This piece of glass is half clear and half silvered, to allow some light to pass through.

Eyepiece
The user looked at the horizon through this and the clear part of the horizon mirror.

Scale
The curved scale is marked in degrees.

Arm
This was moved until the Sun or a certain star appeared to just touch the horizon.

Magnifier
A magnifying glass helped the navigator read the scale.

Chronometer
A chronometer is a very accurate timepiece. Navigators used it to help determine their longitude. Ordinary clocks, which do not work accurately in extreme conditions, would be affected by the rolling of a ship.

Local time
The time recorded was compared to the time in, for example, London.

Countdown to disaster

On the fourth day, *Titanic* reached its fastest speed so far. Ahead lay an ice field 78 miles (125 km) wide, so other ships slowed or stopped, and they radioed warnings. But *Titanic* roared into the dark night on Sunday, April 14.

5 AM

Up all night

Marconi operators Jack Phillips and Harold Bride finished repairing *Titanic*'s radio. The all-night repairs had left them exhausted, but they started tapping out the huge pile of waiting messages.

A TYPICAL RADIO ROOM

12 NOON

Ship's position

Officers used a sextant to determine *Titanic*'s position. They found that the ship had traveled 546 miles (880 km) in 24 hours, at an average speed of 22.06 knots (25.4 mph / 40.1 kph)—its best day yet.

SEXTANT AND MAP

5:50 PM

The ship changed course to be in line for New York.

7 PM

High speed

Three boilers, lit that morning, were connected to the engines, which now worked at full power.

BOILERS FIRED UP

5 AM • 8 AM • 11 AM • 2 PM • 5 PM

White dots represent 3-hour increments.

Sunday morning

Lifeboat drill canceled

Captain Smith canceled a lifeboat drill—nobody is sure why. This meant that the launch of two lifeboats in Southampton was the only time the crew had practiced the complicated procedure.

LIFEBOATS ON DECK

9:12 AM

An ice warning was received from Caronia.

11:40 AM

An ice warning was received from Noordam.

1:49 PM

An ice warning was received from Amerika *but not sent to the officers on the bridge.*

1:54 PM

An ice warning from Baltic *was given to Captain Smith, who later handed it to Bruce Ismay.*

6 PM

Ismay showed the ice warning to two women as he chatted with them.

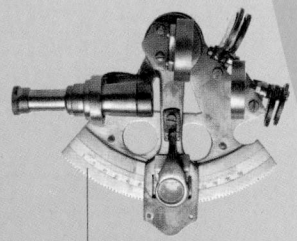

Sextant

Early arrival?

Throughout lunch, excited passengers speculated about whether the speeding *Titanic* would reach New York on Tuesday night rather than Wednesday morning.

APRIL 1912

S	M	T	W	T	F	S
	1	2	3	4	5	6
7	8	9	10	11	~~12~~	~~13~~
14	15	16	17	18	19	20
21	22	23	24	25	26	27
28	29	30				

[Too fast]

Eyewitness

NAME: Charlotte Collyer

LIVED: 1880–1914

FROM: Basingstoke, UK

DETAILS: Collyer was traveling second class with her husband and daughter. After dinner on Sunday evening, a stewardess warned her that there could be icebergs ahead. Collyer recalled the stewardess's words.

"[This] is a dangerous part of the ocean. Many accidents have happened near [here]. . . . Icebergs drift down as far as this."

10 PM

Missing

New officers started their shifts, and lookouts Frederick Fleet and Reginald Lee climbed up to the crow's nest. They did not have binoculars—these had been misplaced.

11:40 PM

Collision

Lookout Fleet rang the brass bell three times and yelled down the telephone: "Iceberg right ahead." The ship turned hard to starboard to try to avoid it, but 37 seconds later, *Titanic* struck a giant iceberg.

7:30 PM
Officers made careful observations of the stars to pinpoint the ship's position.

9:25 PM
Captain Smith went to his cabin.

9:30 PM
Officer Lightoller telephoned the lookouts to remind them to keep a sharp eye out for ice.

11:30 PM
Cyril Evans, the only radio operator on Californian, *switched off for the night.*

11:35 PM
Titanic *thundered along at 22.5 knots (26 mph / 42 kph), its fastest speed so far.*

8 PM — **11 PM** — **11:40 PM**

7:22 PM
An ice warning was received from Californian, *which had stopped.*

7:37 PM
Titanic *was so close to* Californian *that its radio overheard an ice warning sent to another ship.*

8:55 PM
Captain Smith left the dining room and talked with Lightoller on the bridge.

9:52 PM
Mesaba *warned of icebergs and pack ice. Jack Phillips did not send the message to the bridge.*

11:07 PM
An ice warning from Californian *boomed into Phillips's headphones. Busy and annoyed, he tapped out, "Shut up! Shut up!" He did not tell the bridge.*

7:10 PM

Ice warning noted

Captain Smith received *Baltic*'s warning telegram back from Ismay so that it could be noted in the chart room.

CAPTAIN SMITH

BRUCE ISMAY

Eyewitness

NAME: Charles Lightoller

LIVED: 1874–1952

FROM: Hampshire, UK

DETAILS: Second Officer Lightoller later said that if he had seen *Mesaba*'s message, the disaster might not have happened.

"Without a shadow of doubt, I should have slowed her down at once . . . and sent for the captain. More than likely, . . . he would have stopped the ship altogether and waited for daylight to feel his way through."

su

* How did the crew escape the flooded rooms?
* What hit the seabed first?
* Whose dog took a place in a lifeboat?

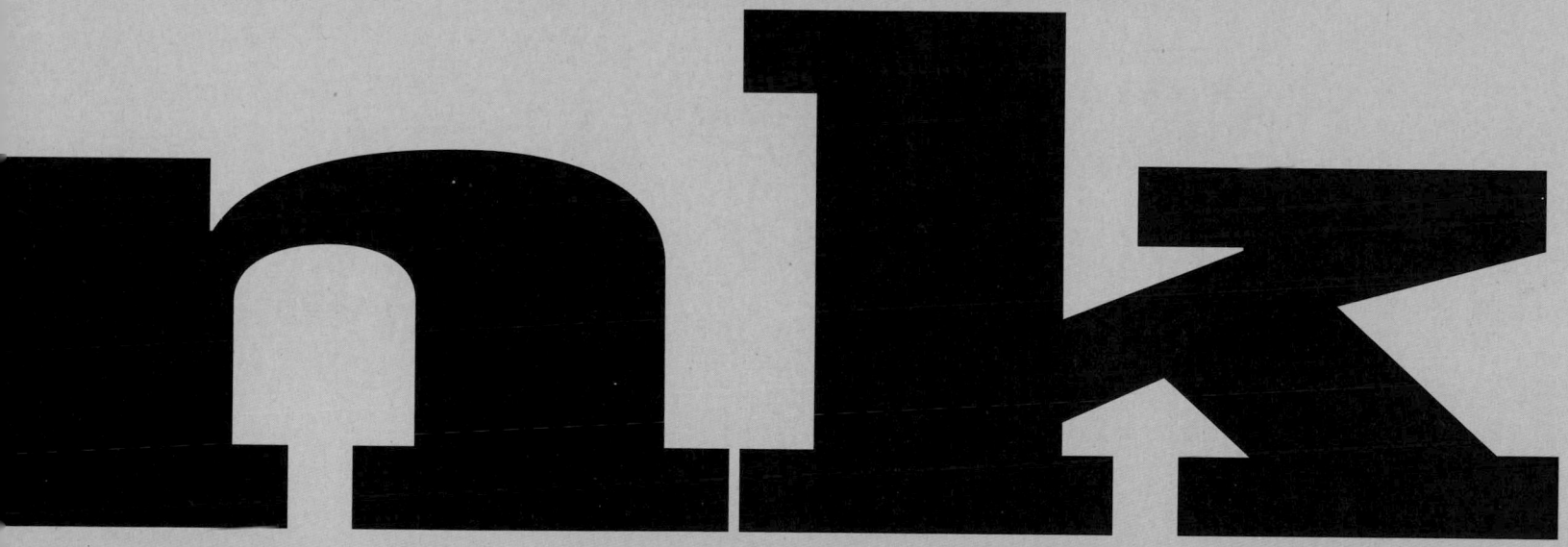

Ice monster

This may be the very iceberg that *Titanic* struck. The ship hit the iceberg at 11:40 PM. At the time, nearly all the passengers were asleep, so they did not realize what had happened. But some woke as chunks of ice crashed onto the deck, and others woke when they heard the iceberg scraping the side of the ship. Minutes later, an eerie silence fell on *Titanic*—its engines had stopped.

Damage [11:40 PM–12:45 AM]

For up to an hour after *Titanic* hit the iceberg, most of the passengers had no idea how much danger they were in. Below them, stokers (firemen) fought a flood.

Making jokes
Relaxed passengers joked that Captain Smith wanted to repaint the damaged hull before sailing on!

Noisy steam
Escaping steam was so loud that people had to shout to be heard.

Confusion on deck

At 12:05, Captain Smith ordered the crew to prepare the lifeboats. Since Smith had canceled lifeboat practice, some of the crew did not know where to go or what to do.

Eyewitness

NAME: Eva Hart
LIVED: 1905–1996
FROM: London, UK
DETAILS: Hart's father wrapped seven-year-old Eva in a blanket and carried her to the boat deck.

"[My father] said: 'They are going to launch the boats. Purely a precaution; you will all be back on board for breakfast.' . . . He put my mother and I in a lifeboat and he didn't make any attempt to get in himself."

Why didn't passengers get in lifeboats?

- Not everyone knew the way to the boat deck.
- It was freezing, noisy, and confusing on deck.
- Many third-class passengers spoke no English.
- Passengers felt safer on *Titanic* than in lifeboats.
- There were no loudspeakers to make announcements.

Smoke and steam

After the collision, the engines were shut down immediately. Steam had to be released from the boilers so that they did not explode. The steam was fed into pipes on the sides of the funnels.

Lifeboat prep

It took about 20 minutes per boat to remove the cover, plug the hole that let out rainwater, and arrange the ropes to swing the boat out over the ocean.

SCENE FROM THE MOVIE *TITANIC* (1997)

Time line: First hour

11:40 *Laughing passengers kicked and threw chunks of ice that had broken off the iceberg and landed on the decks.*

11:41 *The ship was still and silent for the first time on the trip. Soon after, the boilers started to let off steam noisily.*

11:55 *Mail clerks waded through knee-high water to rescue floating mailbags, hauling them up to the sorting room.*

12:15 *The band played, to try to keep passengers calm. This might have led some to think that the situation was less serious than it was.*

Rockets launched
Distress rockets soared high into the sky, where they exploded into white stars.

Waterway
Rivets burst and water flowed between the plates of the hull.

Hissing pipes
These warned the crew that air was being pushed out by incoming water.

Radio rescue attempt

At 12:15, Captain Smith asked senior radio operator Jack Phillips to start sending distress messages. Harold Bride helped Phillips as he pounded the transmitter.

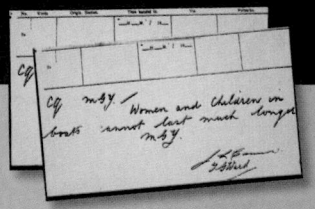

Marconigrams
Any messages received were handwritten on special forms.

Lifesavers

As the compartments flooded, the crew had to climb emergency ladders to escape, because the watertight doors were locked.

SCENE FROM THE MOVIE *A NIGHT TO REMEMBER* (1958)

Eyewitness

NAME: Frederick Barrett

BORN: 1884

FROM: Southampton, UK

DETAILS: Barrett was the leading stoker for boiler room 6. He was standing in the coal bunker when the iceberg opened up a steel plate in it. Barrett scrambled up a ladder over the watertight doorway as it closed, returning minutes later to try to rescue his trapped workmates.

"Water came pouring in 2 feet [0.6 m] above the stokehold plate; the ship's side was torn. . . . We did go back, but we could not go in there because there were about 8 feet [2.4 m] of water."

12:25 DISTRESS MESSAGE FROM *TITANIC*:

"We have collision with iceberg. Sinking. Can hear nothing for noise of steam."

PHILLIPS TAPPED OUT THIS MESSAGE MORE THAN 15 TIMES IN A ROW, SHOWING HIS INCREASING PANIC.

12:25 *Thomas Andrews told Captain Smith it was possible that* Titanic *could sink in less than two hours.*

12:30 *The crew loaded women and children onto Lifeboat 7. Many preferred to stay on deck rather than swing out over the sea.*

12:45 *The first lifeboat—less than half full—began its jolting journey 60 feet (18 m) down toward the dark water.*

12:45 *An exploding distress rocket alerted passengers to the fact that the ship truly was in great danger.*

In distress [12:45 AM–2:17 AM]

As lifeboats were lowered and the waters rose, people on *Titanic* realized that not all of them would be saved.

Pray with me
Father Thomas Byles said prayers with passengers at the aft end of the boat deck at 2:10.

Last chance
At 2 AM, four men played their last hand of cards at their usual table.

Lucky Lady

Margaret Hays was traveling first class with two old school friends. She had her tiny Pomeranian dog, Lady, with her. Hays wrapped Lady in blankets and carried her as they boarded Lifeboat 7, the first to be launched. Lady was one of only three dogs that survived.

A POMERANIAN

Lifeboats

The crew strictly enforced the practice that, in case of emergency, women and children should be evacuated first. Officers did allow a few men to climb in, and others jumped in as boats were winched down.

Eyewitness

NAME: Ida Straus

LIVED: 1849–1912

FROM: Germany

DETAILS: Straus and her husband could have joined her maid on Lifeboat 8, but her husband would not leave with women and children still on *Titanic*.

"I will not be separated from my husband. As we have lived, so will we die together."

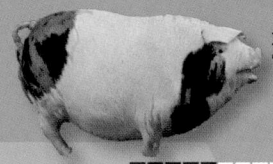

EDITH'S TOY PIG

Heavy landing
A man jumped in, landed on Annie Stengel, and broke her ribs.

Dog on board
This boat included Henry Harper with his wife, servant, and Pekingese dog.

Female driver
English aristocrat the Countess of Rothes steered this boat.

Payload
This was the boat on which Sir Cosmo Duff Gordon paid the crew (see page 97).

12:45 AM: LIFEBOAT 7

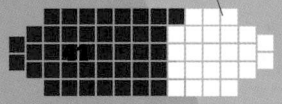

12:55 AM: LIFEBOAT 5

12:55 AM: LIFEBOAT 3

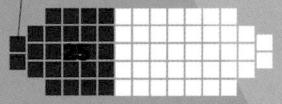

1 AM: LIFEBOAT 8

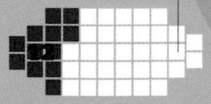

1:05 AM: LIFEBOAT 1

Lifeboat launch time line
The number of passengers on each lifeboat is shown in the red area of the boat.

Pig tune
Edith Rosenbaum played her toy musical pig to comfort children nearby.

Hide me
Daniel Buckley hid under a woman's shawl after other men were removed.

Near miss
This boat descended fast and nearly landed on Lifeboat 13.

Women only
Officer Lightoller ordered a group of men off this boat.

Window access
Passengers climbed into this boat through the windows of the promenade.

1:35 AM: LIFEBOAT 11

1:40 AM: LIFEBOAT 13

1:40 AM: LIFEBOAT 15

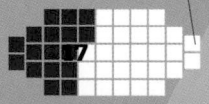

1:45 AM: LIFEBOAT 2

1:45 AM: LIFEBOAT 4

Last songs
The band played ragtime tunes and hymns on the deck outside the gym.

Lifeboats
The forward funnel broke off at 2:17, crushing some people but washing others to safety.

Launch site
Distress rockets were fired from the bridge about every five minutes.

Wave save
The collapsible canvas-sided boats A and B were stuck until a wave washed them into the water.

Third-class passengers
The passengers from the boat had their cabin in steerage moved in. They crammed their belongings and headed all or up to higher decks.

Eyewitness

NAME: Nellie Becker
LIVED: 1876–1966
FROM: South Bend, IN
DETAILS: Becker's son Richard, age one, and daughter Marion, age four, were put on Lifeboat 11, but not her daughter Ruth, age twelve. Becker cried out:

"Please let me in this boat! Those are my children! . . . Ruth! Get in another boat!"

A PISTOL LIKE THE ONE LOWE FIRED

Warning shots

Officer Harold Lowe saw a group of men by Lifeboat 14. "They were glaring more or less like wild beasts, ready to spring," he said. He fired his gun to warn them off. Other officers may have done the same.

Major help
Major Arthur Peuchen slid down a rope to help sail this boat.

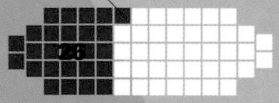

1:10 AM: LIFEBOAT 6

Left behind
Benjamin Guggenheim is said to have watched this boat leave, then dressed in his best clothes to die.

1:20 AM: LIFEBOAT 9

Officer in charge
Harold Lowe took charge of this boat himself.

1:20 AM: LIFEBOAT 14

Class divide
Unusually, all passengers on this boat were second or third class.

1:20 AM: LIFEBOAT 16

Jumper
A man jumped into this boat as it was lowered past B Deck.

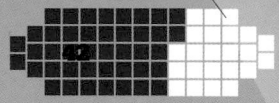

1:25 AM: LIFEBOAT 12

Lucky catch
A French woman fell as she boarded this boat and was caught by her ankle.

1:50 AM: LIFEBOAT 10

Star traveler
White Star boss Bruce Ismay got on this boat.

2:00 AM: COLLAPSIBLE C

Human wall
The crew linked arms to keep men off this boat.

2:05 AM: COLLAPSIBLE D

Wave power
The crew struggled to launch this boat; then a wave swept it out.

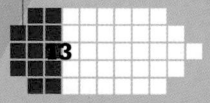

2:15 AM: COLLAPSIBLE A

Overturned
A wave swept this collapsible off the ship upside down.

2:15 AM: COLLAPSIBLE B

Key
- Passenger
- Empty spot
- Overload

The last lifeboat

Lifeboat D was the last lifeboat to be launched from *Titanic*, at 2:05 AM. As the boat was lowered, two men jumped the 9-foot (3 m) gap from A Deck, just making it into the boat.

The occupants watched *Titanic* sink minutes later and said the Lord's Prayer as they floated in the freezing darkness. At dawn, Officer Harold Lowe, in Lifeboat 14, saw them struggling—they did not have enough passengers who could row. Lowe towed them 4 miles (6.5 km) toward *Carpathia*.

Passengers and crew included:

- Quartermaster **Arthur Bright**, who helped fire the distress rockets and loaded passengers into lifeboats before taking charge of this one.
- **Michel** and **Edmond Navratil**, two young French boys who lost their father in the disaster (see page 104).
- Five-year-old **Michael Joseph**, the other child on board, who was reunited with his mother on *Carpathia*.
- **Joseph Duquemin**, a third-class passenger who persuaded the crew to take him in from the water because he could row. He developed terrible frostbite, and his legs were later amputated.
- **Caroline Brown**, who took the last spot on the boat when her friend Edith Evans told her, "You go first. You have children waiting at home." Evans did not survive.
- **Frederick Hoyt**, who put his wife, **Jane Hoyt**, on board before the lifeboat was lowered, then jumped into the sea and climbed in, too.

Safety in sight
The flimsy canvas sides of Lifeboat D are clearly visible in this picture, taken at 7:15 AM as the lifeboat neared the rescue ship *Carpathia* after five hours at sea. Arthur Bright is at the back, using an oar as a rudder.

All alone [No help]

Radio distress messages alerted ships on the Atlantic to *Titanic*'s plight. Captain Smith hoped for help, but he knew it was too late—the ship was sinking fast.

Ships in the area

Titanic was in a busy shipping lane, and there were other boats in the area. When *Titanic* called for assistance, *Californian* was the only ship that did not try to help (see pages 98–99).

Ice field
Any rescue mission would need time to sail around the ice field.

LENGTH OF ICE FIELD: 78 MILES (125 KM)

RMS *TITANIC*
41.46 N 50.14 W

17 miles (27 km) away
SS *Californian*
Sailing from London to Boston, its crew spotted *Titanic*. But *Californian* stopped in the ice field overnight and her radio operator went to bed.

"Women and children in boats. Cannot last much longer."
—JACK PHILLIPS, RADIO OPERATOR

50 miles (80 km) away
SS *Mount Temple*
Heading from Antwerp, Belgium, to Boston, this ship was blocked by the ice field.

50 miles (80 km) away
SS *Parisian*
Parisian, sailing from Scotland to Halifax, Canada, could not pass the ice field.

79 miles (127 km) away
SS *Birma*
This slow steamer sailing from New York to Rotterdam, the Netherlands, was blocked by ice.

N
W
E
S

58 miles (93 km) away
RMS *Carpathia*
Carpathia was a Cunard liner sailing from New York to eastern Europe. Captain Rostron dodged icebergs to sail for *Titanic* at full speed.

Get ready
Rostron turned off his ship's heating to increase power to its engines, and he prepared to receive survivors.

Too far to help

Among the ships that were too far away to help was *Titanic*'s sister ship *Olympic*. The radio station at Cape Race, Canada, sent out messages seeking ships that were closer to *Titanic*.

RMS *Olympic*
500 miles (800 km) southwest, sailing from New York to Southampton

SS *Frankfurt*
140 miles (225 km) southwest, first to reply to *Titanic*'s distress calls

Cape Race
380 miles (610 km) west, a radio station for relaying messages

Last calls

Senior radio operator Jack Phillips frantically tapped out messages as *Titanic* sank. Below are some of his calls for help, and the replies. The two positions given for the ship are incorrect.

Tapping out Morse code

Radio communication was new in 1912. It took some time to send and receive messages, because they were tapped out in a code made up of dots and dashes.

12:15 **CQD *Titanic* 41.44 N 50.24 W.**

12:17 **CQD CQD SOS *Titanic* position 41.44 N 50.24 W. Require immediate assistance. Come at once. We struck an iceberg. Sinking.**

12:20 **Come at once. We have struck a berg. It's CQD OM. Position 41.46 N 50.14 W.**

12:25 *Carpathia*: Shall I tell my captain? Do you require assistance?

12:26 **Yes. Come quick.**

12:32 *Carpathia*: Putting about and heading for you.

1:10 **We are in collision with berg. Sinking head down. 41.46 N 50.14 W. Come soon as possible.**

1:27 **We are putting the women off in the boats.**

1:45 **Come as quickly as possible OM. Engine room is filling up to boilers.**

2:17 **CQ—** (Then the signal stops as the power fades.)

Too late

At 12:25 AM, Captain Smith (standing) knew that it would take four hours for help to arrive—but *Titanic* would have sunk by then.

Watch your back

The two radiomen worked until there was no more power. Assistant Harold Bride went to get Phillips's coat. He returned to find a stoker trying to steal Phillips's life jacket off his back. They punched the thief, ran to the deck, and leaped off the sinking ship.

Jack Phillips

He worked the radio nonstop until the power failed.

Harold Bride

He jumped from *Titanic* into the water with Phillips.

Key to abbreviations

CQD = Emergency (an older distress signal)
SOS = Emergency (a new signal, adopted in 1906)
OM = Old man (a standard phrase at the time)

More here

For key to symbols, see page 112.

Samuel Morse Morse code **North Atlantic ice field** radio waves **radio station** SS *Californian*

"Nearer, My God, to Thee," "Our God, Our Help in Ages Past," and **"There Is a Green Hill Far Away"** were among the popular hymns probably played by *Titanic*'s band as the ship sank.

Learn about *Titanic*'s radio room and its operators at www.hf.ro.

Read the ice warnings from other ships at www.titanic-titanic.com/warnings.shtml.

ice field: a large expanse of ice on the surface of the ocean, consisting of many ice floes and covering an area that is greater than 6 miles (10 km) across.

Morse code: a code used for transmitting messages, in which letters and numbers are represented by short or long signals.

radio: an electronic device designed to transmit and receive radio signals.

"Men, you have done your full duty. You can do no more. Abandon your cabin. Now it's every man for himself."
—CAPTAIN SMITH TO THE RADIOMEN, 2:05 AM

Final moments [Breakup]

It took three years to build *Titanic*, and four minutes for it to sink. At 2:17 AM, the bow sank below the surface, and the ship plunged to the seabed with 1,500 people still on board.

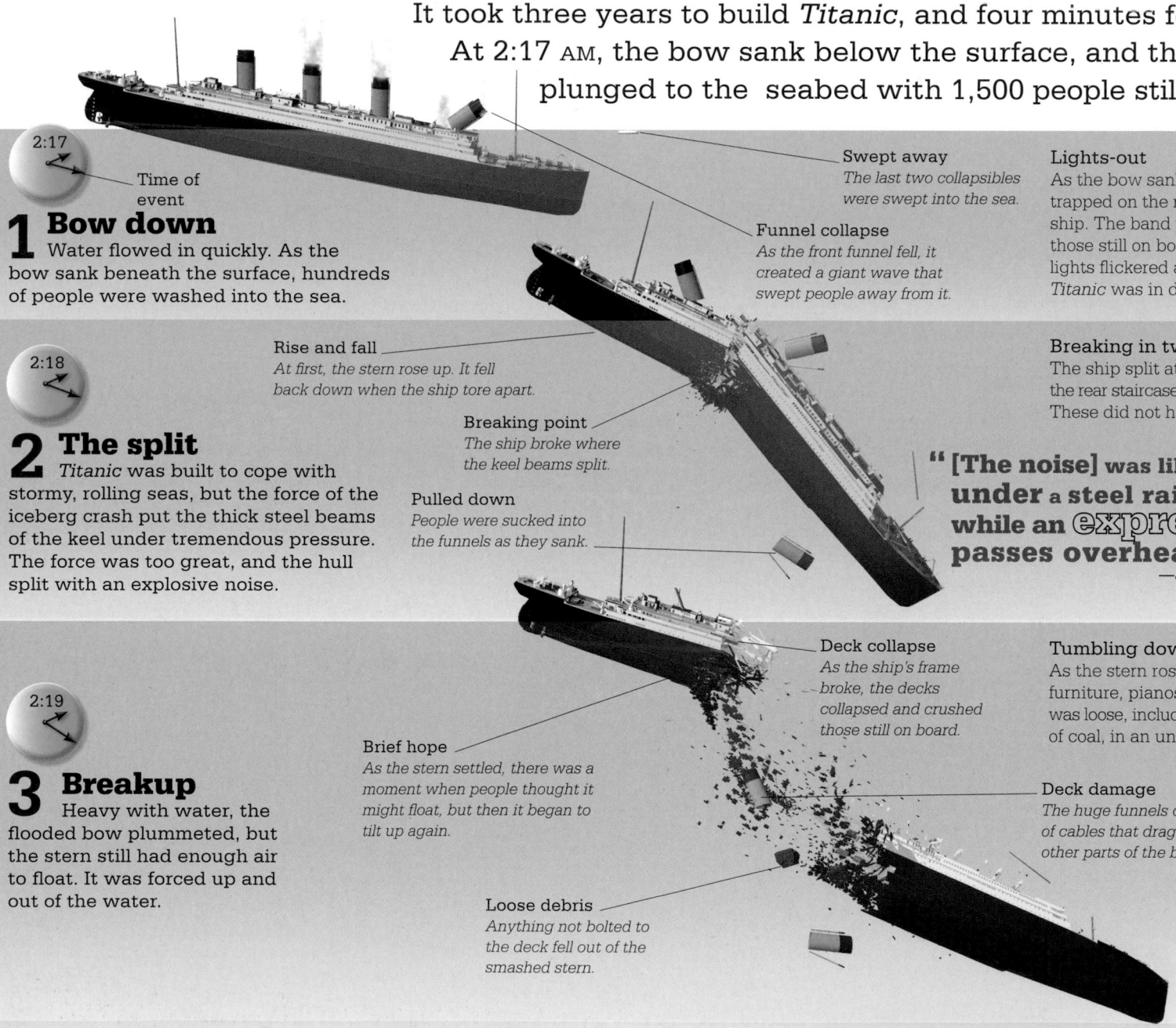

1 Bow down

Water flowed in quickly. As the bow sank beneath the surface, hundreds of people were washed into the sea.

Lights-out
As the bow sank, people were still trapped on the rear decks of the ship. The band played on to calm those still on board. Then all the lights flickered and went out, and *Titanic* was in darkness.

2 The split

Titanic was built to cope with stormy, rolling seas, but the force of the iceberg crash put the thick steel beams of the keel under tremendous pressure. The force was too great, and the hull split with an explosive noise.

Breaking in two
The ship split at its weakest point, at the rear staircase and the engine room. These did not have strong supports.

> **"[The noise] was like standing under a steel railway bridge while an express train passes overhead."**
> —JACK THAYER, FIRST-CLASS PASSENGER

3 Breakup

Heavy with water, the flooded bow plummeted, but the stern still had enough air to float. It was forced up and out of the water.

Tumbling down
As the stern rose, it tipped out furniture, pianos, and anything that was loose, including thousands of tons of coal, in an underwater avalanche.

4 Final plunge

The stern was pushed upright and spun around before it followed the bow, plunging 12,144 feet (3,701 m) straight down to the seabed.

Falling apart
Within minutes, the two sections of *Titanic* crashed into the seabed. They landed about 2,000 feet (610 m) apart, because the bow fell at an angle of about 12 degrees, while the stern dropped vertically, like a lead weight.

Titanic came to rest on the seabed

Eyewitness

NAME: Charles Lightoller
LIVED: 1874–1952
FROM: Southampton, UK
DETAILS: Lightoller was second officer on *Titanic*. After he organized the loading of the lifeboats, he was pulled into the water from the ship.

"Striking the water was like a thousand knives being driven into one's body, and, for a few moments, I completely lost grip of myself. . . . Suddenly a terrific blast of hot air came up the shaft, and blew me right away from the air shaft and up to the surface."

Stepping out
Chief baker Charles Joughin held on to a rail and stepped into the water as the boat sank.

Corkscrew course
The rudder swung to one side, making the stern spiral as it sank.

Vertical stern
The stern floated upright for about a minute. Then it slid gently into the waves.

Air pockets
As air trapped in the stern was forced out, the hull was torn apart.

Hatch crash
The forward hatch cover blew off and landed 200 feet (60 m) from the bow.

Speeding bow
The bow smashed into the seabed at about 23 mph (37 kph), sinking 60 feet (18 m) into the mud.

Shattered plates
The large steel plates that covered the hull broke off as the ship was torn apart.

Debris field
Thousands of objects falling from Titanic were scattered across an area of about 2 square miles (5.2 sq km).

Last chance

As *Titanic* sank, collapsible Lifeboat B was washed upside down into the freezing sea. Radioman Harold Bride found himself in an air pocket beneath it, and he managed to climb onto the overturned hull. He joined 30 other people who were standing on the boat or clinging to its sides. The boat sank lower in the water as the air pocket leaked away, and waves washed over the survivors as the boat rocked. Some of them died, and their bodies slipped into the dark water. Officer Charles Lightoller instructed the desperate group to lean against the direction of the rolling to keep the boat afloat through the night.

Meanwhile, Fifth Officer Harold Lowe moved people from Lifeboat 14 into another boat and gathered a crew of eight men to look for survivors. He was afraid that their boat would be turned over if too many people tried to climb in, so he waited. At about 3:20 AM, he returned. His lamp shone on a mass of dead bodies held up by their life jackets. Lowe hauled four more people aboard, but one died almost immediately. Lifeboat 14 was the only one of *Titanic*'s lifeboats that went back in search of survivors (see page 99).

Desperate struggle
The scene of survivors climbing onto the overturned Lifeboat B was re-created for the 1958 film *A Night to Remember*.

Lost found

* Why couldn't Harold Bride walk off *Carpathia*?

* What did US senators say about the sinking?

* Who received money to return to England?

and

find

Rescued [Terrible wait]

Carpathia found *Titanic*'s lifeboats floating among huge icebergs in the early morning of April 15. The cold survivors were taken on board, and the liner sailed to New York. Soon the tragic story of the sinking and the massive loss of life became a worldwide sensation.

Rescue ship
Carpathia's public rooms became dormitories, and the three dining rooms were used as first-aid stations, one for each class.

Long wait

Lifeboat 2 was the first to reach *Carpathia*, at 4:10 AM. It took hours to find the other boats and bring 707 people on board. Sadly, 3 people had died on the lifeboats, and another died on *Carpathia*.

All lost
Carpathia's passengers donated clothing and helped treat the shocked, freezing survivors after their terrifying night in open boats.

Confusion

During the four days of *Carpathia*'s journey to New York, survivors' names were radioed to land and released to the public. But this took time. Meanwhile, newspapers ran stories that were often sensational and inaccurate.

Messages home
It took days for operators on *Carpathia* to radio the names of survivors.

Newspaper frenzy
Journalists, eager for exclusive news, offered big money to tell survivors' stories.

Who survived?
New York crowds were desperate for news. No one knew how *Titanic* could have sunk.

Eyewitness

NAME: Charlotte Collyer

LIVED: 1880–1914

FROM: Basingstoke, UK

DETAILS: Like many wives taken to *Carpathia*, Collyer hoped her husband had survived.

"We could only rush frantically from group to group, searching the haggard faces, crying out names. . . . I had a husband to search for. . . . I had believed [he] would be found in one of the boats. He was not there."

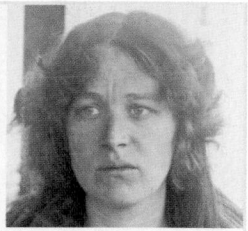

CHARLOTTE COLLYER

Crippled by the cold
Radio operator Harold Bride (center) had to be carried from the ship because he could not walk on his frozen, bandaged feet. The *New York Times* paid $500 for his story.

Late arrival

Carpathia arrived in New York at 9:30 PM on April 18. Each passenger class left separately, and it was 11 PM before third-class survivors touched dry land.

Families fear the worst

A crowd studies the list of *Titanic*'s survivors, posted outside White Star's Southampton office. Families waited days for news, and a local reporter said that he "heard many a sad story of loved ones aboard the ill-fated vessel, who in many cases were the breadwinners of the family." More than 720 of *Titanic*'s almost 900 crew members were from Southampton, and all but 3 were men. Only 124 returned.

Saved and lost [Too many]

Of the 2,223 people on *Titanic*, only 706 reached New York—most of them women and children. Many families were left without husbands and fathers to support them. The crew's pay was stopped. Here, find out what happened to some of the people you met earlier in this book.

Saved

"Women and children first" meant that 75 percent of the women and 50 percent of the children lived. The crew members who were in charge of sailing the lifeboats also survived.

MARGARET BROWN
(See page 49.)

HAROLD LOWE
(See pages 60, 79, and 81.)

STUART COLLETT
(See page 54.)

Charlotte Collyer
Collyer and her daughter received relief funds and $300—equivalent to $6,000 today—for a magazine article, which helped them return to England. (See pages 71 and 91.)

Douglas Spedden
Young Spedden and the rest of his family were saved. (See pages 66–67.)

Archibald Gracie
Gracie was dragged down "in a whirlpool of water, swirling round and round." A strong swimmer, he fought his way to the surface and found a spot in a lifeboat. (See page 98.)

***TITANIC* CREW AT COURT BEFORE THE UK INQUIRY**

Poor crew
Their pay stopped the second *Titanic* sank, so much of the crew had to appeal to the public for funds.

706 saved; 1,517 lost (crew and passengers)

EVA & ESTHER HART
(See pages 55 and 76.)

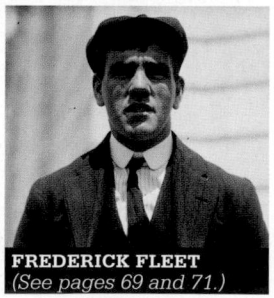

FREDERICK FLEET
(See pages 69 and 71.)

JOSEPH BOXHALL
(See page 60.)

Lost

Some people put loved ones on lifeboats, then stayed on *Titanic*. Others, such as Jack Phillips, found a boat but died at sea. Every death was a tragedy.

JACK PHILLIPS *(See pages 70–71, 77, and 83.)*

Benjamin Guggenheim
This millionaire put on his fine clothes and said that he and his valet were "prepared to go down like gentlemen." (See pages 53 and 79.)

Thomas Andrews
Titanic's designer did not try to save himself and was last seen staring at a picture in the first-class smoking room. (See pages 34 and 77.)

Isidor and Ida Straus
Ida Straus refused to leave her husband to take a place in a lifeboat, so both died. (See pages 52 and 78.)

Death duties
All the musicians died, and their families were billed for lost uniforms.

THE GOODWIN FAMILY *(See pages 56–57.)*

SIDNEY GOODWIN AND HIS SHOES

Sidney Goodwin
Sidney was the 19-month-old baby left out of the family picture at above right. The whole family died, and Sidney's shoes are now in a museum.

JOHN STARR MARCH
(See page 58.)

WILLIAM MURDOCH
(See page 60.)

Numbers
Survivors are shown in the top bars; those who died are below.

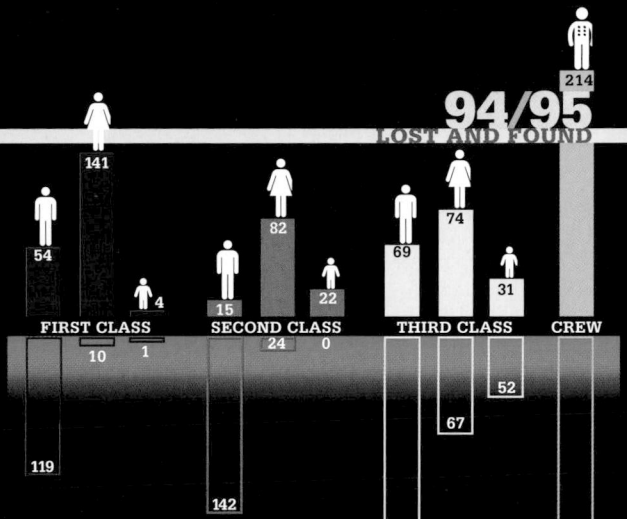

Class divide

It is hard to determine who lived and who died, because papers were lost at sea. These numbers are the ones confirmed at the US inquiry (see pages 96–97). Passengers on the upper decks had a better chance of reaching the lifeboats. Crew members sailing the boats rescued some of their shipmates from the sea.

Hugh McElroy
When he knew all was lost, the chief purser shook hands with his shipmates and said, "Well, good-bye, fellows. It looks like sand for breakfast tomorrow." (See pages 60 and 64.)

Lost crew
Engineers died trying to save the ship by keeping the water from pouring in.

British inquiry
The inquiry, from May 2 to July 3, 1912, concluded that the sinking was "brought about by the excessive speed at which the ship was being navigated."

Heroes and villains

Two inquiries and hundreds of newspaper stories cast some of *Titanic*'s passengers and crew as heroes or villains. Many of the survivors sold their stories to the press, and some gave evidence at the inquiries.

Heroes

Amazing stories of people's calm bravery in the panic and confusion of *Titanic*'s final hours emerged. Officer Charles Lightoller helped passengers onto lifeboats, then fell into the sea near an overturned collapsible. He was the last survivor to board *Carpathia*. Other heroes were passengers who helped steer boats or stepped off lifeboats to make room for others.

John Jacob Astor
Barred from his wife's lifeboat, Astor called out to comfort her as her boat was lowered.

Countess of Rothes
Noël Leslie steered Lifeboat 8 all night long, unlike others who let the crew do the work.

Officer Charles Lightoller
Lightoller (right) helped people off the ship, then kept a lifeboat afloat in the sea, saving more.

US inquiry
US Senate committees set up an inquiry and held hearings from April 19, reporting to Congress on May 28. Both the British and the US inquiries came to the same conclusion: If Stanley Lord, captain of the *Californian*, had gone to *Titanic*'s assistance when the first distress rocket was seen, many lives would have been saved.

[Praise and blame]

Villains

The media named three main villains: Stanley Lord, captain of the *Californian* (see page 99); Cosmo Duff Gordon, a passenger who was accused of bribing crew; and Bruce Ismay, one of *Titanic*'s owners, who got into a lifeboat and left others to die. He said, "I took the chance when it came to me."

Bruce Ismay
Ismay was condemned as a coward by the press and the public after he saved himself.

Cosmo Duff Gordon
Duff Gordon gave the crew on his lifeboat $25 each, supposedly as a bribe to not row back for survivors.

Captain Smith: hero or villain?

Opinions were divided over *Titanic*'s captain. Was he to blame for speeding into an ice field, or a hero for organizing the lifeboats without saving himself?

"His indifference to danger was one of the direct and contributing causes of this unnecessary tragedy."

—SENATOR WILLIAM ALDEN SMITH, TALKING ABOUT CAPTAIN SMITH AT THE US INQUIRY ON MAY 28, 1912

"He was doing only that which other skilled men would have done in the same position."

—SIR JOHN CHARLES BIGHAM, AT THE BRITISH INQUIRY, POINTING OUT THAT CRUISING AT HIGH SPEED AT NIGHT WAS THE USUAL PRACTICE

"Had Capt. Smith been on the bridge, I am confident that the horrible accident would have been averted. . . . At seven o'clock on the night of the accident the captain went to a dinner party in full dress and stayed until nine or ten-thirty, and I am at a loss to understand why a captain with 2,000 souls in his care, and in a ship approaching icebergs, should dine in a restaurant in that way."

—MAJOR ARTHUR PEUCHEN, FIRST-CLASS PASSENGER, IN A NEWSPAPER INTERVIEW

Smith memorial
This statue honoring Smith is inscribed with his alleged last words: "Be British."

Big questions

Over the years, many books and articles have been written about the night that *Titanic* sank. Theories have been proposed and arguments have raged about exactly how and why the disaster occurred. At least four big questions remain.

Big story
This eastern European stamp, depicting an artist's impression of *Titanic*'s sinking, shows that the story of the disaster was known around the world.

The ice warnings question

Ice ahead
It was unusual to find ice as far south as *Titanic*'s route.

Should Captain Smith have paid more attention to the ice warnings from other ships?
Keep in mind that the route was farther south than where icebergs normally floated, and the warnings that officers received did not mention ice directly ahead. Also, one message never reached the bridge at all, because the radio operators were so busy.

"There had been an extremely mild winter in the Arctic, owing to which, ice from the ice cap and glaciers had broken away in phenomenal quantities. . . . In my fifteen years' experience . . . I had certainly never seen anything like it."

—OFFICER CHARLES LIGHTOLLER, IN HIS 1935 AUTOBIOGRAPHY, TITANIC *AND OTHER SHIPS*

"With the atmosphere literally charged with warning signals and wireless messages registering their last appeal, the stokers in the engine room fed their fires with fresh fuel, registering in that dangerous place her fastest speed."

—SENATOR WILLIAM ALDEN SMITH, AT THE US INQUIRY ON MAY 28, 1912

The speed question

Should *Titanic* have been moving more slowly?
It sped through the night at 22.5 knots (26 mph / 42 kph). But this was a normal speed for transatlantic liners, which had tight deadlines to meet. However, on that night, other transatlantic ships had slowed down or even stopped because of the ice warnings.

"Towards evening the report, which I heard, was spread that wireless messages from passing steamers had been received advising the officers of our ship of the presence of icebergs. . . . No diminution of speed was indicated and the engines kept up their steady running."

—COLONEL ARCHIBALD GRACIE, FIRST-CLASS PASSENGER, IN HIS 1913 BOOK, *THE TRUTH ABOUT THE* TITANIC

"Every captain who has run full speed through fog and iceberg regions is to blame for the disaster as much as [Captain Smith] is: they got through and he did not."

—LAWRENCE BEESLEY, SECOND-CLASS PASSENGER

The *Californian* question

Could *Californian* have helped? *Californian* was the ship nearest to *Titanic* at the time of the sinking. It had lifeboat spaces for 218 people and could have shuttled many more passengers to safety. But the radioman had gone to bed. *Californian*'s crew spotted *Titanic*'s distress rockets, but the captain, Stanley Lord, said that he thought they were a greeting between ships from the same company.

The ship on the horizon
Passengers and crew on *Titanic* saw the lights of a ship on the horizon. Captain Smith told the lifeboats to row toward it, but the ship disappeared from sight. It was *Californian*.

"When we passed one of our own steamers, we would salute them by firing a distress rocket. . . . It was the height of every shipmaster's ambition in those days, and officers and crew too, to pick up a ship in distress. . . . If we'd had any sign of anything like that, we'd have been after it like a shot."

—CAPTAIN STANLEY LORD

CAPTAIN LORD

Sea regulations at the time stated that if a ship saw "rockets or shells, throwing stars of any color or description, fired one at a time, at short intervals," it must offer help to the ship in distress.

The US inquiry concluded that *Californian*'s "officers and crew saw the distress signals of the *Titanic* and failed to respond to them."

The lifeboats question

Why didn't the lifeboats collect more passengers from the water? There weren't enough lifeboat seats for everyone on board *Titanic*, and in the confusion many boats were launched only half full. Then the lifeboats were rowed away quickly, to avoid being sucked down with *Titanic*. Hundreds of people still on *Titanic* were thrown into the freezing water as the ship sank, but only one lifeboat returned to help.

"As soon as the ship disappeared I said: 'Now, men, we will pull toward the wreck.' Everyone in my boat said it was a mad idea because we had far better save what few I had in my boat than go back to the scene of the wreck and be swamped."

—HERBERT PITMAN, THIRD OFFICER

"There they were, only four or five hundred yards away, listening to the cries, and still they did not come back. If they had turned back several hundred more would have been saved."

—JACK THAYER, FIRST-CLASS PASSENGER

Last of the boats
Carpathia carried some of *Titanic*'s lifeboats to New York Harbor and dropped them off at the Cunard pier there.

Found [Miles down]

The broken wreck of *Titanic* lay scattered across the seabed for 73 years. No one knew exactly where it was or had the right equipment to search so deep.

Detailed study
In 2004, Ballard used two underwater robots, steered from a ship floating above.

Film crew
This robot camera had powerful lights to film in the dark.

Hard to find

The last position given by *Titanic* before it sank was wrong, so explorers could only guess the correct location of the wreck. And it lies too deep underwater for divers to reach alone.

Wreckage trail

Marine scientist Robert Ballard found *Titanic*. He searched for debris by towing an unmanned deep-sea vehicle, equipped with cameras, from a ship.

***Alvin* the submersible**
Ballard visited the wreck site in *Alvin*, a deep-sea diving craft that held crew.

1985 French scientists, working with Ballard, dragged a scanner near the wreck site and found the debris field.

1986 Ballard visited the wreck in the *Alvin* submersible.

1987 Explorers salvaged objects from the site. This continued for years.

1995 Film director James Cameron filmed the site, using some of the shots in his 1997 movie, *Titanic*.

1998 A large piece of the hull was recovered, two years after the first salvage attempt had failed.

2010 The whole site was mapped using sonar.

Effects of time

Titanic is falling apart. Sea creatures have eaten most of the wood. Metal is being destroyed by salt, water pressure, and rust. And bacteria and fungi hang from surfaces like icicles.

Robbing a grave?

Dives into the *Titanic* wreck have brought thousands of artifacts to the surface. These include plates and cups, as well as items that belonged to the dead. Some people consider this robbing a grave.

Explorers took more than
6,000
objects from the site

Surviving items
Clothes, glasses, bags, and watches are all that remain of those who died on *Titanic*.

POCKET WATCH

GLADSTONE BAG

Sea view
These are the windows of a first-class cabin on the port side of the boat deck.

EYEGLASSES

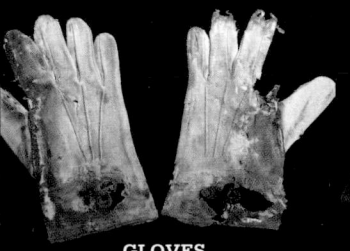

GLOVES

VEST

All that remains
This pair of boots marks where a body landed. Only the leather footwear survives.

More here

For key to symbols, see page 112.

***Finding the* Titanic**
by Robert D. Ballard

***Secrets of the* Titanic**
is a 1986 documentary about finding the wreck.

***Deep Inside the* Titanic**
is a 1999 film that explores the wreck site.

"It Was Sad When that Great Ship Went Down" is a folk song about the sinking. Other songs include **"The Wreck of the *Titanic*"** by Jeff Calhoun, from 1927, and **"Down with the Old Canoe"** by the Dixon Brothers, from 1938.

Visit **Titanic** in Branson, MI, which is a replica of the ship, and **Titanic** in Pigeon Forge, TN, which also exhibits artifacts in a ship-shaped museum.

salvage: to recover something from a wreck.

sonar: a method of finding underwater objects by reflecting sound waves off of them.

submersible: a vessel that can travel underwater.

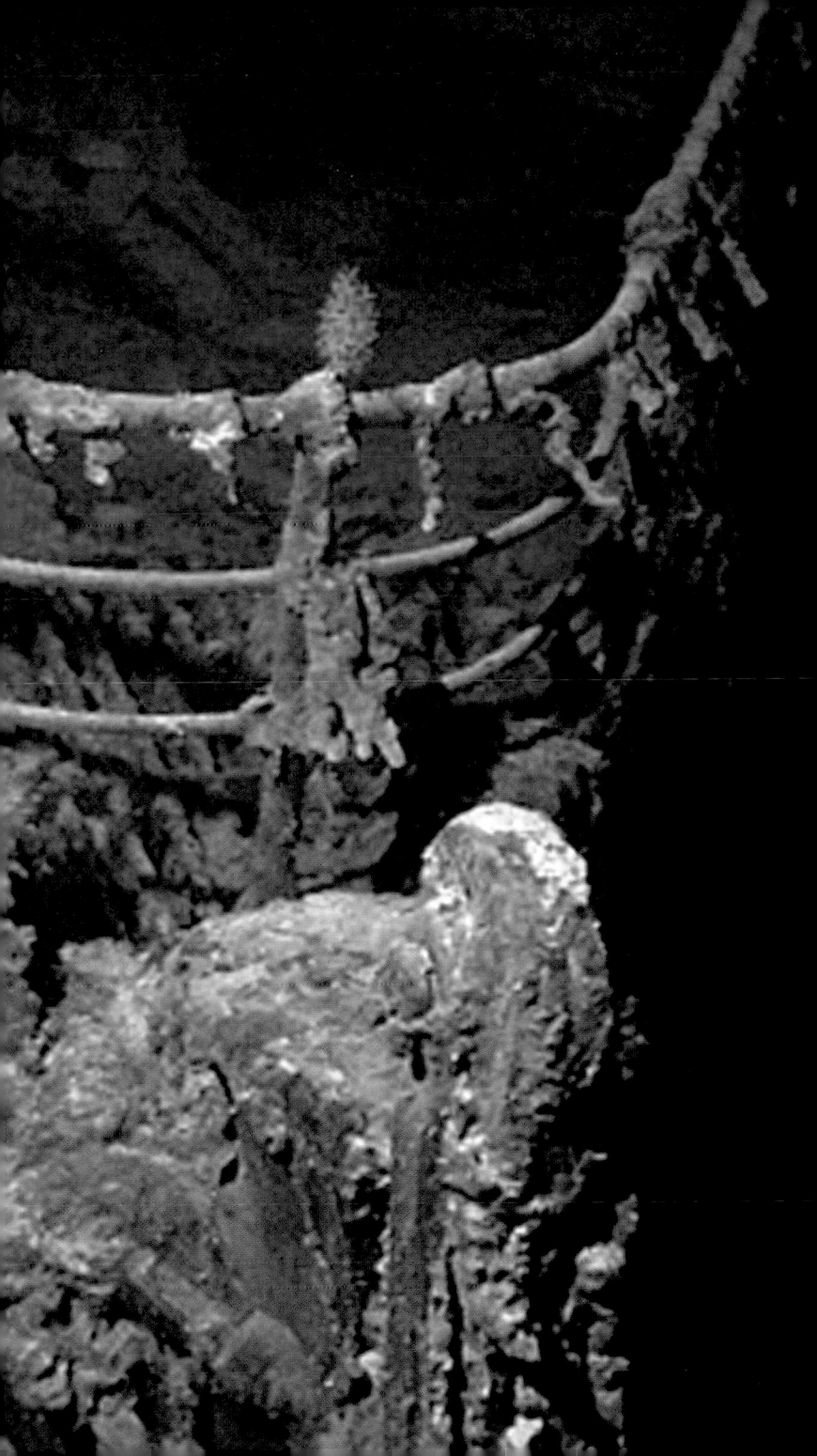

At rest

This is *Titanic*'s bow. It fell 2.3 miles (3.7 km) to the seabed, where its sharp edge plunged into the silt like a knife. Microbes have eaten away at the steel plating on the hull and created strangely shaped rust formations. This photograph was taken in 2004 by scientists on a research expedition.

Survivors [Amazing stories]

The survivors of *Titanic* were affected by the disaster forever. Some became celebrities, others lost everything, and many had to start new lives alone.

Orphans of the deep

Michel Navratil had separated from his French wife and kidnapped their sons. He gave them false names on *Titanic*— Loto and Louis Hoffman (see p. 54)— so when he died, no one knew who the boys were. Newspapers called them the "orphans of the deep."

Reunited
Newspaper reports eventually reached their mother, Marcelle, and she was reunited with her sons in New York on May 16.

Navratil brothers
Michel was three and Edmond was two when they were rescued (see p. 81). Survivor Margaret Hays looked after the boys in New York.

Starring role
Leading actress Dorothy Gibson played herself in a film about the sinking, made just four weeks later. In the movie, Gibson wore the same white silk dress she had worn on the night of the disaster.

Lost a fortune
Madeleine Astor (see pages 49 and 59) inherited a fortune when her husband died on *Titanic*. She survived, and gave birth to their son. But four years later she gave up the money to marry again.

Sportsman in love
Tennis star and first-class passenger Karl Behr married Helen Newsom a year after the sinking. He had followed Newsom onto *Titanic* to persuade her to marry him.

Last survivor
Millvina Dean was a baby on *Titanic*, traveling third class. Her mother and brother survived, but her father died. Later she became known for appearances at *Titanic* events. She was the last survivor to die, in 2009.

Road casualty
The Spedden family (see pages 66–67) made it to New York, but young Douglas died in 1915 after being struck by a car.

The ship that survived
Another survivor was *Titanic*'s sister ship *Olympic*. Fitted with extra lifeboats and proper watertight compartments, it served as a liner until 1935. During World War I, it was used as a troopship and earned the nickname "Old Reliable."

Left behind
Two years after the sinking, Lucile Carter divorced her husband. He had boarded a lifeboat and left her for dead on *Titanic*.

Glossary

aft
Close to or toward the stern, or rear, of a ship.

apprentice
A person learning to do skilled labor. Some apprentices were legally bound to an employer or craftsman for a period of time in order to learn a trade.

aristocrat
A person who is a member of the highest social class in a particular society.

ballast
Heavy material, such as gravel, sand, or iron, that is placed in the bottom of a ship to stabilize it. The ballast may be redistributed or removed to change its effect on the movement of the ship.

bankrupt
Lacking money and unable to pay off any debts.

berth
A place to sit or sleep on a ship. A two-berth cabin has two beds in it.

boilermaker
A person who makes or repairs boilers or other heavy metal items.

bow
The front end of a ship.

breadwinner
A person who supports a family with his or her earnings.

bribe
To persuade someone to do something by offering or promising money or a gift.

bridge
The platform from which a ship is piloted and navigated.

bunker
A large container or compartment for storing fuel such as coal.

cargo
Goods or merchandise carried on a ship.

chart
A map used by navigators on a ship to determine its course.

chauffeur
A person employed by a wealthy person or family to drive a car.

chronometer
A very accurate clock that is not affected by the movement of a ship or by changes in air pressure, temperature, or the atmosphere.

compass
An instrument for finding direction, usually with a magnetized needle that turns on a pivot and points to the magnetic north.

crow's nest
A partly enclosed platform at or near the top of a ship's mast, used by a lookout to spot approaching danger.

current
A steady flow in a particular direction in a body of water.

davit
A cranelike machine used to raise and lower objects such as lifeboats over the side of a ship or a hatchway.

debris
The remains of something that has broken up.

disembark
To go ashore from a ship.

draftsman
A person who draws plans of machinery that will be built.

dry dock
A place where a ship is repaired or painted. After the ship has sailed into the dry dock, the water in the dock is pumped out. The dock is filled with water again when the ship is ready to leave.

emigrant
A person who leaves his or her country to live in another country.

engineer
A person trained in the design, construction, and use of engines or machines.

evacuate
To remove from a dangerous place to somewhere safer.

famine
A serious lack of food

TITANIC IN DRY DOCK

in a region because of a disaster such as war or a drought.

firn
Grainy snow on the upper part of a glacier, where it has not yet been compressed into ice.

forge
To heat and hammer metal in order to change its shape.

found
To establish a new company.

founder
To fill with water and sink.

frostbite
The freezing of parts of the body, usually the ears, nose, fingers, and toes.

funnel
A metal chimney on a steamship through which smoke and exhaust gases from the boilers escape.

gantry
A bridgelike overhead structure with a platform that supports equipment such as cranes. A gantry acts as a supporting framework while a ship is being built.

glacier
A slow-moving river of compacted ice, formed by layers of snow that build up on mountains or near the North and South Poles.

greaser
A person who greases, or lubricates, a ship's engines.

hull
The main body of a ship, not including the masts, sails, rigging, engines, or other fittings.

ice field
A large expanse of ice on the surface of the ocean, consisting of many ice floes and covering an area that is greater than 6 miles (10 km) across.

immigrant
A person who comes to live and work permanently in a foreign country.

inquiry
An official investigation into an accident or event, often held in a public place.

isolate
To keep a sick person separate from other people.

keel
A long piece of wood or metal that runs along the bottom of the hull of a ship like a backbone. The ship's frames are attached to it.

latitude
Distance north or south of the Equator, measured in degrees. Imaginary lines of latitude are drawn horizontally around the globe.

life jacket
A buoyant vest hat keeps a person afloat in water.

liner
A large, luxurious ship operated by a shipping company along a regular route.

logo
A symbol or picture that identifies a company or product.

longitude
Distance east or west of the prime meridian—an imaginary line that runs vertically through Greenwich, England—measured in degrees. Lines of longitude are drawn on the globe from the North Pole to the South Pole.

maiden voyage
The first journey of a new ship.

marconigram
A message sent via a Marconi radio.

migration
The movement of people across land or oceans to find new places to live or work.

Morse code
A code used for transmitting messages, in which letters and numbers are represented by short or long signals. The code was invented in 1838 by Samuel Morse.

navigator
An officer on a ship who finds the way from one place to another by using the Sun, the stars, and special instruments.

persecution
A campaign of hostility and ill treatment conducted because of the politics, race, or religious beliefs of a person or group.

port
The left-hand side of a ship when looking forward, toward the bow.

porthole
A window, usually round, in a ship's hull.

poverty
The state of being very poor and unable to buy food or other essential items.

prejudice
A hostile opinion about or attitude toward people of other races or religions. Prejudices are usually formed unjustly, without accurate information or proper reasoning.

promenade
A public place for strolling for pleasure or display. Promenades were very popular in Europe at the beginning of the 20th century.

WATCH RECOVERED FROM *TITANIC*'S WRECK

propeller
A central shaft with attached blades that rotate as the shaft turns. This movement drives a ship forward in water.

purser
An officer on a ship who deals with financial matters and keeps accounts. He looks after money and valuables for passengers and is responsible for their comfort and welfare. The chief purser on *Titanic* was in charge of the stewards.

"It was truly a lovely ship and at that time we felt very lucky to have been able to book passage on her."

—ROBERTHA JOSEPHINE WATT, SECOND-CLASS PASSENGER, AGE 12 WHEN SHE TRAVELED

quartermaster
An officer who steers a ship and has other navigational duties, including signaling.

quoits
A game in which circles of rope are thrown at a target.

radio
An electronic device designed to transmit and receive radio signals through the air via radio waves. It converts electric impulses into sound.

rivet
A metal bolt that holds two or more metal plates together. The bolt is passed through a hole in each plate and then beaten or pressed down when in place.

rudder
A flat, hinged piece of wood or metal used to steer a ship. This underwater blade is positioned at the stern of a ship. When it is turned, it causes the ship's bow to turn in the same direction.

salvage
To recover something from a wreck.

sextant
A navigational instrument used to determine the latitude and longitude of a ship at sea and to set its course. It measures the angle between the horizon and the Sun, the Moon, or a particular star or pattern of stars.

shift
A working period of several hours. Shifts enable different groups of workers to do the same job at different times of the day.

shuffleboard
A game in which standing players use long cues to push wooden disks into numbered areas marked on a smooth surface, such as the deck of a ship.

slipway
A sloping surface that runs down into water. Slipways are used to launch or land ships when building or repairing them.

sonar
A method of finding underwater objects. It involves sending out pulses of sound, then detecting and measuring their return after they have been reflected off other objects. *Sonar* stands for *SOund NAvigation and Ranging*.

starboard
The right-hand side of a ship when looking forward, toward the bow.

stern
The back end of a ship. The stern is at the opposite end of the ship from the bow.

steward
A man whose job is to look after passengers on a ship. A woman who does the same job is called a stewardess.

stoker
A person who stokes, or feeds, a furnace with fuel such as coal in order to run the engines of a ship. On British ships, a stoker is sometimes called a fireman.

submersible
A vessel that can travel underwater. Submersibles are often used for research and exploration.

taffrail log
An instrument used to calculate the speed of a ship through the water. A rotating device is attached to a reading unit and towed through the water from the railing at the ship's stern.

tenement
A run-down and often overcrowded apartment building, usually in a poor section of a large city.

transmitter
The part of a radio that converts sound waves into electric waves.

trimmer
A person who works in the engine room of a ship, shoveling coal and delivering it to the stokers.

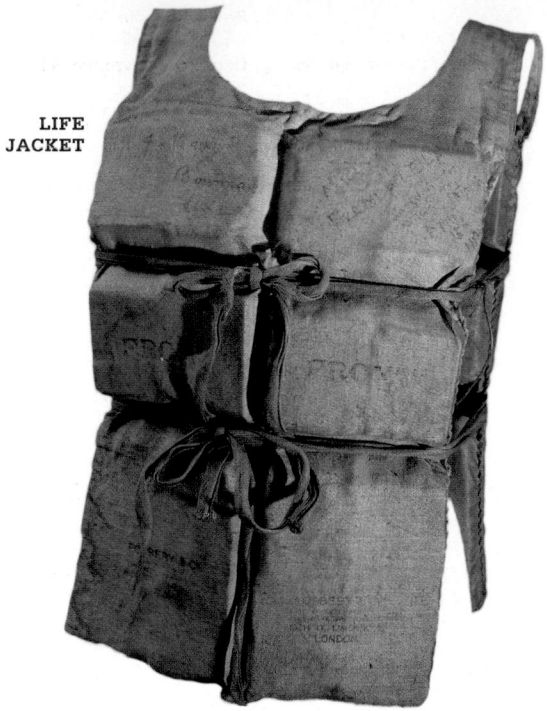

LIFE JACKET

turbine
A wheel with blades that, when spun rapidly, drives a machine to make electricity.

Turkish bath
A bath in which the bather visits a series of steam rooms of increasing temperature, then takes a cold shower and has a massage.

valet
A male servant who looks after his wealthy employer, including taking care of his clothing.

"Don't be so ridiculous. Even if we have grazed an iceberg it can't do any serious damage with all these watertight compartments. . . . Go back to bed and don't worry."

—SIR COSMO DUFF GORDON TO HIS WIFE, LUCY

Index

A

activities, onboard 64, 65, 66–67
A Deck 38, 40–41, 58–59, 66–67, 79, 81
Age of Migration 14
Alvin submersible 17, 100
Amerika (ship) 70
Andrews, Thomas 34, 76, 95
A Night to Remember 14, 15, 77, 87
animals
  dogs 43, 78
  toy pig 78
apprenticeship 34, 35
artifacts 100–101
Astor, John Jacob IV 49, 96
Astor, Madeleine 49, 59, 105
Atlantic Ocean 16, 18, 24–25
  icebergs 26
Aubart, Léontine 53
Australia 20

B

bakery 42, 58
Ballard, Dr. Robert 17, 100
Baltic (ship) 44, 70, 71
barbershop 42, 51, 55
Barrett, Frederick 77
bath, electric 50
bathrooms
  crew 59
  first-class 53
  stewards' 43
  third-class 40, 42, 57
baths, Turkish 43, 51
B Deck 40–41, 58–59, 79
Becker, Nellie 79
bedtime 65
Beesley, Lawrence 41, 54, 98
Behr, Karl 45, 105
Belfast, Ireland 16, 30–31, 35, 38, 39
Belfast News Letter 39
Bigham, Sir John Charles 97
binoculars 69, 71
Birma, SS 82
blacksmith 34
Blue Riband 21
boarding 48–49
boat deck 33, 40–41, 55, 58–59, 76, 78, 101
boilers 36–37, 38, 43, 59, 62, 70, 76
bow 32, 78, 84, 85, 102–103
Boxhall, Joseph 60, 94
Bride, Harold 17, 70, 77, 83, 87, 91
bridge 41, 45, 59, 71, 79, 97, 98
Bright, Arthur 81
Britain
  inquiry 17, 95, 96, 97
  shipbuilding 14, 15, 16, 19, 30–31
Brown, Caroline 81
Brown, Margaret 49, 94
Buckley, Daniel 78
Burns, Elizabeth 67
Byles, Father Thomas 78

C

cabins
  crew 43
  first-class 41, 50, 52–53, 59
  heating in 36, 52
  second-class 36, 54, 55
  shared 43
  suites 50, 53
  third-class 18, 36, 42, 56, 59
cafés 19, 51, 65
  Parisien 40, 59
Californian, SS 71, 82, 96, 99
calving, icebergs 26, 27
Cameron, James 14, 100
Cape Race, Canada 82
captain *see* Smith, Captain Edward John
cargo 40, 42, 43, 62–63
Caronia (ship) 70
Carpathia, RMS
  arrival in New York 17, 91
  distress messages 83
  emigrants 21
  reporting names 17
  rescuing survivors 81, 82, 90 91, 96, 99
Carr, William 63
Carter, Lucile 105
casualties
  artifacts found 100
  from disaster 17, 90, 91, 94, 95
  from shipbuilding 34, 35
cause, of disaster 15, 69, 70, 71, 76, 96–99
C Deck 40–41, 54, 58–59
Chalmers, Sir Alfred 45
chart, navigation 58, 60, 65, 68, 71
Cherbourg, France 48, 49, 53
Chicago 24
children
  games 67
  survivors 94, 95
chronometer 68, 69
church services 57, 59, 78
class system 40, 41, 48
coal
  boilers' use of 36
  during sinking 84
  paddle steamers' use of 18
  shortages 17, 55
  shoveling 61
  storage 62
Collett, Sidney Clarence Stuart 54, 94
Collyer, Charlotte 44, 71, 91, 94
compass 41, 68
construction, of *Titanic* 14, 16, 19, 20, 30–31, 38
  workforce for 30, 34–35, 36
cooks 61, 85
counterweight 31
crane
  shipbuilding 31, 32
  on *Titanic* 39, 40
crew
  after disaster 76, 77
  casualties 95
  lifeboats 81
  number of 60
  pay of 34
  social order of 60
  survivors 93, 94, 95
  on *Titanic* 40, 41, 42, 59
  work times 64
crockery 56, 65, 100
crow's nest 41, 68, 71
Cunard 16, 19, 20, 21
Cunard, Samuel 21

D

daily schedule 64–65
davits 38, 59
D Deck 40–41, 58–59
dead reckoning 68
Dean, Millvina 17, 105
deck
  boat 41
  collapse of 84
  games 65, 67
  layout of 40–43
  promenades 10, 23, 51, 54, 59, 67
  staircases 58
  windows 19, 39
designer of *Titanic see* Andrews, Thomas
dining saloons
  first-class 41, 51, 59
  mealtimes 64
  officers 60
  second-class 40, 55, 59
  third-class 43, 56, 57, 59
disaster
  cause of 15, 69, 70, 71, 76, 96–99
  countdown to 70–71
  hour following 76–77
  inquiries 17, 95, 96, 99
  lifeboats launched 78–79
distress messages 77, 82, 99
distress signals 77, 79, 81, 96, 99
dogs 43, 78
draftsmen 34, 35
drinks 62
dry dock 38, 39
Duff Gordon, Lady Lucy 45, 50–51
Duff Gordon, Sir Cosmo 50–51, 78, 97
Duquemin, Joseph 81

E

eastern Europe 25, 56, 98
E Deck 42–43, 58–59
electricity 14, 21, 30, 36, 38, 42, 50, 51, 53
elevators 40, 41, 51, 55
Ellis Island 24, 25
emigrants 16, 24–25, 49, 56
engineers 61
engines
  shut down 75, 76
  Titanic's 36, 38, 42, 43, 70
  turbines 18, 21, 42
entertainment, onboard 65, 67
Europe, emigrants from 16, 18, 24–25, 49, 56

F

famine 14, 24
fares
  first-class 51
  second-class 54, 55
  third class 18, 57
F Deck 42–43, 58–59
films, about *Titanic* 14, 15, 87, 101, 105
fines, for workers 35
firemen *see* stokers
first class
  boarding 48, 49
  entertainment 65, 67
  escape chances of 78
  facilities 40–41, 42, 50–53, 59
  fares 51
  mealtimes 65
  promenades 10, 59, 67
  service 50
  survivors 95
first voyage *see* maiden voyage
Fleet, Frederick 69, 71, 94
food 40, 56, 59, 60
  cooks 61, 85
  lack of 25
  mealtimes 64, 65

storage 39, 42
supplies 62
forecastle deck 41
forge 34, 35
frame, steel 16, 30, 32, 33, 84
Francatelli, Mabel 45
Frankfurt, SS 82
funnels
breaking off of 79, 84
fitting of 31, 38

G

games, onboard 65, 67
gantry 16, 30, 32
Gatti, Luigi 61
G Deck 42–43, 58–59
Germany 25
Gibson, Dorothy 105
Giglio, Victor 53
glaciers 24, 98
gold rush 20
Goodwin family 57, 95
Gracie, Archibald 94, 98
greasers 61
Great Britain, SS 18
Great Western, SS 18
Greenland 26
guarantee group 34, 35
Guggenheim, Benjamin 53, 79, 95
gym 41, 50, 51

H

Hakkarainen, Elin 57
harbor 18
Harland and Wolff 16, 20, 30–31, 34–35, 36
Harper, Henry 78
Hart, Eva 55, 76, 94
Hawke (ship) 38
Hays, Margaret 78, 104
heater 36, 51, 53
heroes 96
hinges 31
Hoffman, Loto and Louis
see Navratil, Michel and Edmond (children)
horizon mirror 69
hospital 40, 41
Hoyt, Frederick and Jane 81
hull
breaking up of 84, 85
building of 32–33
damage to 76
painting of 38, 39
piece salvaged from 100
shape of 18
human error 15, 96
Hungary 21

I

icebergs 26–27
hit by *Titanic* 17, 26, 71, 75, 76–77
ice field 15, 83
cause of disaster 97, 98
navigation through 69
radio warnings about 15, 17, 68, 69, 70–71, 98
rescue ships 82
immigration, to United States 14, 16, 24–25, 56
International Mercantile Marine Co. 16, 20
interpreters 56
Ireland
building of *Titanic* 16, 30–31
emigrants from 25, 49
Queenstown 48, 49, 62
Ismay, J. Bruce 20, 70, 71, 79, 97
Ismay, Thomas 16, 20
Italy 25

J

jib 31
Joseph, Michael 81
Joughin, Charles 85

K

Kaiser Wilhelm der Grosse, SS 19, 21
keel
breaking in two 84
building of 16, 32
Kemish, George 61
kennels 43

L

laborers, pay 34
largest ship 14, 19
Laroche, Joseph 54
latitude 68
launch of *Titanic* 16, 39
legend of *Titanic* 14, 98
Lenox-Conyngham, Eileen 59
Leslie, Noël 78, 96
library 54, 55, 65
lifeboats
collapsibles 41, 45, 78, 79, 81, 84, 87
davits 38, 59
drill canceled 70, 76
empty seats in 78–79, 99
installation of 38
launch of 17, 76, 77, 78–79, 81, 87
number of 10, 15, 45
position of 10, 40, 41
rescue ships and 90–91
life jackets 44–45, 83
lighting 50, 54, 58, 65, 84
Lightoller, Charles 48, 60
detection of icebergs 69, 71, 98
lifeboats and 78, 85, 87, 96
liners, development of 18–19
living conditions, of immigrants 24, 25
longitude 68, 69
lookouts 41, 68, 69, 71
Lord, Captain Stanley 96, 97, 99
lounges
first-class 41, 51, 64
second-class 55, 64, 65
third-class 57, 64
Lowe, Harold 60, 79, 81, 87, 94
Lusitania (ship) 16, 21
luxury 17, 19, 20, 34, 50, 51, 58

M

magazine report 94
maiden voyage 14, 17, 30, 34, 38, 48–49
mail 20, 21, 62, 76
mainmast 39
March, John Starr 58, 95
marconigrams 64, 77
Marconi radio 39, 41, 61, 70
Mauretania, RMS 16, 19, 21
McCawley, Thomas 50
McElroy, Hugh 60, 64, 95
meals 55, 56, 59, 63, 65
mealtimes 64, 65
See also food
mechanical error 15, 76
Meir, Golda 24
men
casualties 94
escape chances of 78, 79, 81
survivors 95
Mesaba (ship) 71
migration 16, 24–25, 49, 56
Moody, James 60
Moore, Annie 24
Morgan, J. P. 16, 20
Morse code 83
Mount Temple, SS 82
movies 14, 15, 87, 101, 105
Murdoch, William 48, 60, 95
music 40, 59, 65
musicians
casualties 95
playing during sinking 77, 79, 83
rooms of 42
social order of 61

N

navigation 68–69, 70
Navratil, Michel and Edmond (children) 54, 81, 104
Navratil, Michel (father) 104
Newfoundland 26
Newsom, Helen 105
newspaper reports 91, 93, 96, 97, 98
New York
Carpathia in 17, 91, 99
Cunard 21
Ellis Island 24
immigrants in 21, 24
Titanic's arrival in 70
New York Times, the 15, 45, 91
Noordam (ship) 70
Norddeutscher Lloyd (NDL) 19, 21

O

officers
on decks 1–5 40, 41
navigation by 68, 69, 70
social order of 60
Olympic, RMS
after disaster 105
construction of 16, 19, 20
propellers on 8
repairs to 38
sister ship 19, 30
smoking room 51
Titanic's sinking and 82
unsinkability of 45
orlop deck 42–43, 58–59

P

paddle steamers 18
painting 38, 39
Parisian, SS 82
passengers
accommodations 43
activities 65
escape of 77, 78–79
lifeboats launched 76, 77, 78
on maiden voyage 17, 48
reactions to accident 76–77
schedules 64–65
social divisions 40, 64, 79, 90, 91, 95
See also first class; second class; third class
pay
of crew 34, 60, 61, 94
of laborers 34
Pernot, René 53
persecution 14, 24, 25, 56
pets 43, 78
Peuchen, Major Arthur 15, 79, 97

Philadelphia 24
Phillips, Jack 70, 71, 77, 82, 83, 95
Pirrie, Lord William 30, 34
Pitman, Herbert 60, 99
plates, steel 16, 32–33, 77, 85
poop deck 40, 43, 57
portholes 38, 101
position of *Titanic* 68–69, 70, 82, 83, 85, 100
postal clerks 58, 61
postcards 64
post office 43, 58, 61, 62, 76
potato storage 42
poverty 14, 24, 25, 56
Prideaux, Jack 59
promenades
  decks 10, 19, 39, 41, 51, 53, 54, 58, 59, 67, 78
  games 67
  popularity of 23
propellers
  development of 18
  fitting of 38, 39
  on *Mauretania* 16
  sister ship 8–9
  size and weight of 42
purser 60, 64

Q

Queenstown, Ireland 48, 49, 62

R

radio
  distress calls 77, 82–83, 99
  equipment 14, 21, 39, 44
  iceberg warnings 15, 17, 68, 69, 70–71, 98
  messages 64, 70, 77
  operators 17, 41, 44, 61, 70, 77, 83, 95
  survivor information 91
Ranson, Captain John 44
reading and writing room 41, 51
reading unit 68
refrigeration 36, 39, 42
Republic, RMS 44
rescue ships 15, 17, 44, 82, 83, 99
rigging 38
rival lines 16, 20, 21
riveters 16, 33, 34
rivets 33
Rosenbaum, Edith 78
Rostron, Captain 82
rotator 68
Rothes, Countess of *see* Leslie, Noël
Royal Mail 20, 21, 62, 76
rudder 42, 85
Russia 24, 25

S

safety 8
safety measures 19, 43, 44–45
sailboats 18
salvaged objects 100
Scandinavia 25, 56, 57
Scarborough, England 22–23
Scotland Road 43
second class
  cabins 36, 54, 55
  entertainment 65
  facilities 10, 40, 42, 54–55, 59
  fares 54, 55
  mealtimes 65
  service 54
  survivors 95
Servia (ship) 21
sextant 68, 69, 70
Shipbuilder magazine 45
shipbuilding
  in Britain 14, 15, 16, 19, 30–31
  technology 18–19
  workforce 30, 34–35, 36, 38
sinking, of *Titanic*
  causes of 15, 71, 76, 96
  final moments 84–85
  time of 17, 84, 85
sister ship *see Olympic*, RMS
slaughterhouse 42
Smith, Captain Edward John 60, 64
  confidence of 15
  during iceberg danger 15, 70, 71, 98
  inquiry findings 97
  lifeboat drill 70
  ordering distress messages 77, 82, 83
  ordering lifeboats launched 76
  statue of 97
Smith, Senator William Alden 97, 98
smoking rooms
  first-class 51, 64
  second-class 55, 64
  third-class 56, 57, 64
social division
  of crew 60
  of passengers 40, 48, 64, 79
  of survivors 90, 91, 95
Southampton, England
  Cunard line 21
  maiden voyage from 14, 17, 30, 48, 49
  survivor notices in 93
  Titanic's sail to 39
specie room 43
Spedden family 67, 94, 105
speed, of travel 15, 21, 70, 96, 97, 98
squash court 51, 59, 65
staircases 40, 58–59
  grand 41, 51, 58
  second-class 55
  third-class 57
stars, position of 68
staterooms 41, 50, 53
steam, escaping 76
steam power 18, 36, 42
steel
  blacksmiths 34
  body of *Titanic* 32–33, 84, 85
  latticed 31
steerage 18
Stengel, Annie 78
stern, sinking of 84, 85
stewards 60, 64, 65, 71
  bathrooms for 43
  for first-class passengers 50
  pay of 34, 60
  for second-class passengers 54
  in social order 60
  for third-class passengers 56, 59
  waking passengers 78
Stoker, Bram 30, 35
stokers 43, 59, 60, 61, 76, 77, 98
storage 42, 62
Straus, Ida 52, 78, 95
submersibles 17, 100
superliners 21, 30, 45
surgery 40
survivors
  after disaster 104–105
  heroes 96
  life jacket of 45
  notices of 17, 91, 93
  numbers of 17, 93, 94, 95
  rescue of 82, 90–91, 94
  villains 97
swimming pool 43, 51, 54, 58, 65

T

taffrail log 68
tank top deck 42–43, 58–59
technology 14, 15, 18–19, 21, 44
television programs, about *Titanic* 15, 101
Teutonic, SS 18
Thayer, Jack 84, 99
third class
  arrival in United States 24
  dining saloon 43
  escape of 78, 79
  facilities 18, 36, 40, 41, 42, 43, 56–57, 59
  fares 57
  mealtimes 65
  medical inspections 24, 48
  service 56, 59
  survivors 95
time, accurate 69
tips 58, 60, 61
Titanic (film) 14, 76, 100
tools, navigation 68
trains, to *Titanic* 49
transatlantic travel 16, 18, 21, 24–25, 98
trimmers 61, 62
Turkish baths 43, 51

U

United States
  immigration to 16, 18, 24–25, 49
  inquiry 17, 95, 96, 97, 99
unsinkability, of *Titanic* 8, 14, 17, 44–45

V

villains 97

W X

waiters' cabins 43
water, fresh 42, 62
watertight compartments 19, 45, 76, 105
watertight doors 14
White Star Line
  history 16, 17, 20
  logo 56, 65
  shipbuilding 19, 30
  survivor notices 93
Wilde, Henry 60
windows 19, 38, 39, 101
women, survivors 94, 95
workforce
  casualties in 34, 35
  fines for 35
  guarantee group 34, 35
  shipbuilding 30, 34–35, 36, 38
  training 34
  See also crew
work, for immigrants 24
wreck
  discovery of 16, 17, 100–101
  disintegration of 100, 102
  dives to 14, 17, 100
  position of 85, 100
  salvaged objects from 100
  site mapped 100

Y Z

Young, Filson 32

PHOTOGRAPHY AND ARTWORK

Photos ©: Alamy Images: 72 l (AF archive), 77 bl (AF archive), 86-87 (AF archive), 8-9 (ARCHIVIO GBB), 14 inset r (Photo 12), 76 br (Photo 12), 14 inset l (Ronald Grant Archive), 56 bc (Veronika Pfeiffer), 65 bl (Veronika Pfeiffer), back cover l (WENN Rights Ltd); AP Images: 69 br (Alastair Grant), back cover bl, 69 tl, 71 tc, 100 bc, 101 c, 101 bc, 107 (Bebeto Matthews), 56 t (Chitose Suzuki), 58 tl (Eric Risberg), 94 Eva & Esther Hart (Eva Hart), 101 bl (Mary Altaffer), 44 r (Sang Tan), 108 (Sang Tan), 25 br (Stephen Chernin), 61 tc (Tom Gannam); Bridgeman Images: 43 t (Prismatic Pictures); Charles A. Haas: 58 bl, 95 John Starr; Corbis Images: 74-75, 90 bl, 91 tl (Bettmann), 64 bl (F.M. Browne/Bettmann), 45 tr (Hulton-Deutsch Collection), 70 bl (Hulton-Deutsch Collection), 10-11 (Ralph White); Cunard Line: 21 br; Dreamstime: back cover tl, 12 l, 20 (Gorgios), 77 explosion (Pilarts), 34 bc (Tiero), 34 br (Tormentor); Fr Browne SJ Collection:17 tl,41 tc, 48, 48 inset, 49 tr, 50 cl, 62-63, 66-67, 77 cr, 94 Douglas Spedden, 105 br; Getty Images: 19 t (De Agostini Picture Library), 7 l, 12 r, 22-23 (Hulton Archive), 69 tr (Hulton Archive/Stringer), 98 cl (Hulton Archive/Stringer), 91 tc (Hulton Deutsch), 7 cr, 14-15, 64 t (Popperfoto), 100 br (Ralph White), 88 c, 96-97 (Stock Montage), 50 far r, 94 Poor Crew, 97 tc (Topical Press Agency/Stringer), 20 inset, 71 br, 95 Death duties, 97 tl (Universal Images Group); iStockphoto: 64 icons (4x6), 65 bugle (Batman2000), 27 bl (bbuong),65 icons and throughout (bubaone), 76 bl (DanielBendjy), 46 c, 63 br (dja65), 65 sports icons (DusanVulic), 65 quoits (edhor), 71 tr (farbenrausch), 63 bc (FourOaks), 18 icons and throughout (jangeltun), 44 l (jimd_stock), 62 t (JordiRamisa), 65 piano icon (kathykonkle), 78 bl (Laures), 34 cl, 35 cl (LdF), 65 books (Leadinglights), 49 icon (Leontura), 71 cr (Logray-2008), 54 c (mateu), 25 bc (OGphoto), 27 t (pkline), 65 champagne glass (rzymu), 16 br crowd (solid-istanbul), 56 cr (stocksnapper), 65 plates (studiocasper), 98 tr (TonyBaggett), 61 tr (Wulfruna), 62 cb (YinYang), 24 tr (ziggymaj); Joe Knapp: 50 c; Library of Congress: 16 tl (American Stereoscopic Co.), 54 t, 104 (Bain News Service/Flickr Commons Project 2008), 59 tr, 105 tcl (Bain News Service/Flickr Commons Project 2011), 88 r, 91 cr, 94 Charlotte Collyer (Bain News Service/Flickr Commons project 2012 and San Francisco Call, June 2, 1912), 12 c, 24 tl (Detroit Publishing Co. no. 036490/Gift; State Historical Society of Colorado; 1949), 16 cr, 17 tr,46 l,49 br,50 r,54 r,91 tr, 94 Margaret Brown, 94 Stuart Collett, 97 tr (George Grantham Bain Collection), 94 Frederick Fleet (Harris & Ewing Collection), 24 bl (Lewis Wickes Hine), 17 bl,25 bl,88 l,91 b,104 inset; Marko Lulic, Belgrade: cover porthole; Mary Evans Picture Library: 61 l (Interfoto); Mesanthroppee@DeviantArt: 19 ct; National Archives and Records Administration: 72 r,80-81; National Museums Northern Ireland (NMNI): 1, 6, 28 c, 31 cl, 31 bl, 33 tr, 34, 34 bl, 35 b, 36-37, 53 c, 55, 59 br, 64 cb, 70 tr, 95 Thomas Andrews (Harland & Wolff, Ulster Folk & Transport Museum); Navy.mil: 99; Newscom: 7 r, 90-91; NOAA: 100 l,101 t,101 br; RM Auctions: 63 bl (Courtesy of); Royal Museums Greenwich: 56 cl (Bedford Lemere & Co/National Maritime Museum, Greenwich, London), : 78 br (National Maritime Museum Picture Library); Science and Society Picture Library: 61 br, 83 b (Father Browne/UIG/SSPL), 95 Jack Phillips (Father Browne/UIG/SSPL), 21 (NRM/Pictorial Collection), 16 tr (Science Museum); Science Source: 26 bl (Bernhard Edmaier), 26 globe (Claus Lunau/Science Photo Library), 26-27 (Dennis Puleston), 70 tc (Ed Young), 27 bc (GeoEye/Science Photo Library), 68 br (George & Judy Manna), 60 l, 60 tr,94 Harold Lowe, 95 William Murdoch (New York Public Library), 69 bl, 70 bc (Steve Percival), 62 bl (Victor de Schwanberg); Shutterstock: cover b (Alvov), cover bg (Ensuper), 62 ct (Jesus Cervantes), 51 icon and throughout (Leremy), 18 tr, 24 bg, 25 bg, 68 map (Nicemonkey), 55 icons and throughout (oculo), 68 globe icons (SoleilC), cover c (tsuneomp), 71 bg (yienkeat), 4-5, 44-45 (Zacarias Pereira da Mata); Simon Glancey/wwrgallery.co.uk: 19 c,19 cb, 19 b; Southampton City Council Arts & Heritage: 92-93; Swansea Museum: 68 bl; Thinkstock: 26 br (Digital Vision), 18 bl (Hemera), 65 oysters (iStockphoto), 83 tl (Photodisc), 27 br (Photos.com), 65 accordian (Stockbyte); Tim Loughhead/Precision Illustration: 7 cl, 21 tr, 28 l, 31, 32-33, 40-41, 42-43, 46 r, 53 t, 58-59, 68,70 titanic icons, 72 c, 76-77, 78-79, 84, 85, 98 b; Tony Fernandes: 18 cr, 18 br; White Star Photo Library: 2-3, 15 inset l, 16 br, 28 r, 30, 31 tl, 38-39, 40 cl, 40 bl, 41 tr, 41 br, 42 bl, 42 cl, 43 cr, 43 br, 50 bl, 51, 52-53, 54 cl, 54 bl, 56 bl, 56-57 bg, 60 br, 62 br, 64 ct, 64 br, 71 bl, 95 Hugh McElroy, 106; Wikipedia: 96 cl,105 bl (Bain Collection/Library of Congress), 24 br (Bkkbrad), 97 br (Bs0u10e01), 17 br, 102-103 (Courtesy of NOAA/Institute for Exploration/University of Rhode Island (NOAA/IFE/URI), 30 t (CrazyPhunk), 34-35 (Engineering journal: 'The White Star liner Titanic', vol.91), 70 tl (Father Frank Browne), 25 tl (From Preface to the First Edition of An Illustrated History of Ireland from AD 400 to 1800, by Mary Frances Cusack, Illustrated by Henry Doyle), 16 bl (Images of American Political History), 18 c (Johnson, Harry and Lightfoot, Frederick S. (1980): Maritime New York in Nineteenth-Century Photographs, Dover Publications Inc., New York, page 14. From a stereogram by George Stacy), 15 inset r (Le Site du Titanic), 105 tcr (Methods and Players of Modern Lawn Tennis, 1915, (p. 200)/J. Parmley Paret), 33 tl (Miaow Miaow), 100 c (NOAA), 30 l (okänt), 79 cr (Rama), 105 tl (Randy Bryan Bigham Collection), 105 tr (Stephen Daniels), 105 bc (The Day Book (Chicago) 19 April 1912, p. 23), 96 t (The Graphic), 83 tr ("The Wireless Man" by Francis A. Collins, Grosset & Dunlap Publishers, New York, Copyright 1912 by The Century Company), 16 cl (Whistlerpro), 20 bl (Whistlerpro), 61 bc (White Star Line), 21 inset, 49 map, 53 b, 56-57, 82 b, 94 Archibald Gracie, 94 Joseph Boxhall, 95 Isidor and Ida Straus, 95 Sidney Goodwin, 95 The Goodwin Family, 95 Benjamin Guggenheim, 96 c, 96 cr, 99 r, 99 b; Zuma Press: 95 shoes (Wang Lei).

Key to symbols in **More here** columns

Keywords for web searches

Suggested reading

Movies and programs to watch

Songs and recordings to listen to

Exciting places to visit

Great things to do

Mini-glossary

Credits and acknowledgments